"Deb Brede's book is a must read for anyone serious about making good financial choices in retirement—and in life. Part history lesson, part personal experience, part market primer, *You're Retired ... Now What?* packs decades of Deb's wisdom into a small space and reminds us why her clients love her."

—Andy Arnott
President, CEO, and head of wealth and asset management for US and Europe, John Hancock Investments

"Debra Brede tells an incredible story—a true one—of a life and career well lived. Early days in her life became an incredible teacher and disciplinarian that set her up for life and career so well. This book tells that story, while providing great insights, concepts, and practices in wealth management with real life and client examples. Most interestingly and importantly, Debra shows—again by example—the importance, ability, and satisfaction in giving back. Readers will be instructed, motivated, and inspired to act, therefore, like Debra, making the world a better place."

—Bob Doll
Senior portfolio manager and chief equity strategist, Nuveen

"Many obtain success, but few give back unselfishly, and few can match Debra's generosity. She not only gives financially, but she takes time to go to India to spend time with the orphans and help wherever she can! Debra and her husband have volunteered at the Agape orphanage in India for more than twelve years. She came from nothing, has it all by my metrics, and gives sacrificially to those in need. A true modern-day hero. An inspiring read."

—Lynne Voggu
Founder, Agape AIDS Orphan Care

"I have worked with thousands of financial advisors throughout my career. While it would be challenging to label any of them 'the best,' since each offers a unique perspective and serves differing types of investors, none exceeds Deb Brede's unwavering passion for helping her clients achieve their goals. I have known Deb for thirty years and nobody—I mean nobody—outworks her or is more passionate about guiding clients and their families through life's journey

"Deb has taught me a lot about hard work, money management, focus, and client service over these three decades. She brings all of it to life in the pages of *You're Retired ... Now What?*, from stories of her childhood, to the mentors who most influenced her thinking, to explaining the truths and myths of investing, and ultimately to finding one's real purpose and path for a satisfying retirement.

"Readers of this wonderfully written book will gain perspective on the dos and don'ts of investing in general—and on how their choices might affect retirement in particular."

—Wayne Bloom
CEO, Commonwealth Financial Network

I dedicate this book to my husband, Ken Brede, who has been the wind underneath my wings for the last forty-one years; and to my children, Josh and Ashley, who have loved me in spite of the sacrifices they had to make sharing me with my career.

Debra Brede

YOU'RE RETIRED ...

Now What?

DISCOVERING & FUNDING YOUR
purpose-driven retirement

ForbesBooks

Published by ForbesBooks, Charleston, South Carolina.
Member of Advantage Media Group.

ForbesBooks is a registered trademark, and the ForbesBooks colophon is a trademark of Forbes Media, LLC.

Printed in the United States of America.

10 9 8 7 6 5 4 3 2 1

ISBN: 978-1-94663-363-7
LCCN: 2019919319

Cover design by Megan Elger.
Layout design by Wesley Strickland.

This publication is designed to provide accurate and authoritative information in regard to the subject matter covered. It is sold with the understanding that the publisher is not engaged in rendering legal, accounting, or other professional services. If legal advice or other expert assistance is required, the services of a competent professional person should be sought.

 Advantage Media Group is proud to be a part of the Tree Neutral® program. Tree Neutral offsets the number of trees consumed in the production and printing of this book by taking proactive steps such as planting trees in direct proportion to the number of trees used to print books. To learn more about Tree Neutral, please visit **www.treeneutral.com**.

Since 1917, the Forbes mission has remained constant. Global Champions of Entrepreneurial Capitalism. ForbesBooks exists to further that aim by bringing the Stories, Passion, and Knowledge of top thought leaders to the forefront. ForbesBooks brings you The Best in Business. To be considered for publication, please visit **www.forbesbooks.com**.

Contents

Acknowledgments

I want to thank my beloved clients for trusting me with their financial well-being.

I want to thank Anthony Noel for his amazing work in editing and polishing my words in this book. He is a talented editor and writer, and I could not have done this book without his guidance and tireless support.

I want to thank the Lord my God because without him I would not be where I am today.

"But remember the Lord your God, for it is he who gives you the ability to produce wealth."

—Deuteronomy 8:18

Foreword

RETIREMENT IS SOMETHING that's on everyone's mind … eventually. As the time nears, or is thrust upon us, we must face not only decisions about financial realities but also how to enjoy, celebrate, and make the most of this next stage of life. Many people wither in retirement—physically, mentally, and energetically—while others thrive.

The difference is generally a result of proper planning and, just as important, one's attitude. In the words of Albert Einstein, "There are only two ways to live your life. One is as though nothing is a miracle. The other is as though everything is." Sign me up for the happy one! And make no mistake, proper planning can provide the solid foundation for a healthy attitude to more easily thrive.

I've known and admired Debra Brede for most of her career. She's an original, and that's exactly what your retirement should be—custom crafted for your needs and desires, flexible enough to change as you and the world evolve, with a rock-solid foundation to build upon and a functional structure to protect you and your loved ones.

Easier said than done. Given that you probably haven't retired many times before, or even once, it's fair to say that you're a retirement novice. You've worked hard, made some mistakes, and hopefully learned from them. Now it's time to enjoy the fruits of your labor, ratchet down the stress, amp up the joy, and finally realize the dreams you've fantasized about all these years.

But just as with every great new endeavor, retirement has a learning curve, not to mention a few surprises along the way. There are rookie mistakes, and occasionally some bad ones. But retirement also has its share of success stories. So how can you stack the deck in your favor? This is where a trusted guide comes in.

Celebrated by one and all—the financial press as well as her colleagues and clients—Deb Brede isn't just another financial advisor. Commonwealth Financial Network, with whom Deb has been associated for thirty years, is home to two thousand of the best and brightest advisors in the industry. And among this elite group, Deb is perched at the top in terms of the success of her practice ... and has been for many years. How does someone do that? How can one person consistently be among the best of the best?

The answer is simple: Deb Brede possesses the intellect and understanding that allows her to cut to the chase, to find what works, and to execute accordingly. She has no tolerance for sales pitches, only for sensible solutions. And perhaps even more important, she possesses a passion for helping others.

Not surprisingly, her clients love her for it. They depend on her wisdom and they tell their friends about her. Her business has grown by word of mouth, and as you travel the pages of this book and read her stories and understand her process, you'll appreciate why. Like Deb, *You're Retired ... Now What?* is totally to-the-point, insightful, and purpose-driven.

When Deb asked if I would write the foreword for her book, I was honored. However, while I happily agreed to do this because I adore Deb and she has always been an important part of Commonwealth, I didn't anticipate how much I'd delight in reading it.

Frankly, my initial intention was to skim through the manuscript, digest her approach, and write a well-deserved laudatory intro. But I couldn't put it down. Who knew?!

Deb shares her secret sauce and explains exactly what she does and why. In that respect, it's a tutorial for investors and advisors alike. But be warned: if you read this book, you're likely to end up wanting Deb Brede to be your advisor. More importantly, you'll have a much better understanding of what a great advisor feels like.

> *We live in an age where most answers are but a click away. But clearly that's not enough. Retirement is too important a topic to leave to chance. Or to inexperience. The true luxury in today's world is having an experienced and trusted expert in your corner— be it financial, medical, or any other area where you need help and guidance—who knows and cares about you, and who helps you to realize your most important dreams and objectives.*

—Joseph Deitch, chairman and founder, Commonwealth Financial Network

Part One

The Best Teacher

CHAPTER 1

When Planning Meets Reality

Ask any successful person: planning and reality are often two different things.

Countless books have been and continue to be written about planning for retirement. They urge readers to begin the planning process as early as possible, then give the author's take on the best strategies for establishing and increasing a nest egg during the reader's working life. The hope, of course, is that by the time she or he is ready to retire, the reader will have the financial resources they'll need to enjoy their golden years.

That is all well and good for most working people. But I didn't write this book for them.

This book is for high-net-worth people who are either very close to retirement or have already quit working. People for whom having adequate resources in retirement, quite frankly, isn't going to be an issue.

Unless they really screw things up.

Maybe that put a smile on your face, but it's no laughing matter. It actually happens all the time. Having seen it happen since the earliest stages of my career, I made helping people who have amassed significant wealth avoid screwing up my top priority, and it has remained my primary goal for the past thirty-three years.

> It is in execution and adaptation where things can get tricky, especially for people who haven't, like me, devoted their lives to studying and implementing strategies designed to protect and grow wealth.

Over those years, I've seen innumerable market ripples, wrangles, climbs, and crashes. I've worked with hundreds of highly successful people, every one of whom understood—intellectually, at least—a crucial truth: planning alone does not guarantee anything. Only by *executing* our plans and *adapting* them as circumstances change do we create our best chance at living the reality we hope to live in retirement.

Left to their own devices, many of these smart, wealthy people would have tended to make poor decisions. My goal is to help those who lack my hard-won expertise make better choices, and I believe my contrarian approach—which I'll discuss in detail a bit later—helps me do that, each and every day.

It is in *execution* and *adaptation* where things can get tricky, especially for people who haven't, like me, devoted their lives to studying and implementing strategies designed to protect and grow wealth. There's no how-to book for doing that, but even if there were, it would read to the uninitiated as if it had been translated from

Chinese. Into Latin. Or maybe Sanskrit. For reasons which, by the time you've finished *this* book, I think will become clear.

But here's a hint: too many considerations—both fundamental and complex—must be taken into account when the goal is protecting and growing wealth. In learning them, there is simply no substitute for direct experience.

* * *

Without exception, the clients I serve are concerned with three things:

- never running out of money during their lifetimes,

- providing for their survivors after they've passed, and

- preserving and expanding their ability (read: money) to give to philanthropic pursuits aimed at making the world a better place.

In short, I help wealthy, purpose-driven retirees protect and grow the legacies they want to leave their families—and the wider world—after they are gone.

Why me?

But why do they want *my* help? I think it is because I am a bottom-line-driven person.

The simple fact is that planning is only as good as the reality it creates—in other words, whether our plans succeed.

I learned what happens when people lack a plan, let alone the will to follow it, in childhood.

My parents were teenagers when they had me. They were, quite literally, kids raising kids. My grandmother loved to remind us that, at my father's high school graduation ceremony, I was in my mother's belly while my brother sat on my mom's lap. Mom had four kids by her twenty-third birthday. It might have been six, but she lost a set of twins within hours of their birth. My own daughter is almost twenty-five, and I can't imagine her with four kids and lost twins.

Memories of my growing-up years are of my parents fighting. Always about money, because they had none.

"If only they had money," I thought, "they'd stop fighting."

It's impossible to fully appreciate the seriousness I bring to the work I do—the degree to which I hold myself accountable for helping my clients succeed—without first understanding how I grew up.

Tough times

My mom was miserable. She was tied down to raising kids, while her old high school friends could have fun—go to parties, date, and enjoy life. Mom had been very beautiful and popular in high school, when she met my father. The multiple pregnancies did a number on her body, including unsightly varicose veins on her once-gorgeous legs.

Mom blamed us for everything, including the fact that she was overweight—as if all her consecutive pregnancies, lack of exercise, and not eating right had nothing to do with it. (I have never seen my mom eat a vegetable!)

My mom's pregnancies happened before she learned to cook. Her idea of making a spaghetti dinner was opening a can of Campbell's tomato soup and pouring it on overcooked noodles.

My father never came home for dinner. The only dinner I remember eating with him was one Easter, when he brought his mother to our house. All of us kids knew this grandmother hated my mom, as she often told us that my mother trapped my dad into marriage by getting pregnant with my brother, Bruce.

So Mom, in an effort to impress her mother-in-law with a nice Easter meal, bought Swanson TV dinners and baked them. Then she dished the sides into bowls—the peas and potatoes—and the thinly sliced turkey went onto a serving plate. She brought everything proudly into the dining room, as if she'd made it herself. (Technically, I guess, she had.)

When her mother-in-law came into the kitchen for something, as mothers-in-law often do, she spotted the empty boxes in the kitchen waste can. My mother never did live this down, and the incident gave my father's mother, Grandma Cole, one more reason why my mom was not right for my father.

Since Mom did not cook, it was every kid for themselves. My brother Bruce and I took over the job of cooking when we were very young. Our staple was ketchup bread sandwiches, and once in a while a slice of baloney added when my mom had extra money.

We learned to make soups, and always added a lot of water so the broth filled us up. We made "ketchup soup" by boiling a soup bone (which was cheap, as the butcher had removed all the meat). After an hour, we added ketchup for color, then boiled noodles for ten more minutes before serving. Potato soup was one of our favorites, made with a small splash of milk to give color to the broth. (Milk was a precious commodity, and in our house, it was meant for the baby who had most recently arrived. ONLY.)

* * *

After Dad left my mom for another woman, Mom signed us up for paper routes. Bruce and I were too young to get them on our own. I hope you're sitting down: I was five, he was six.

My mother signed us up for one at first, then a second. Together they made a route large enough to produce a decent income—for a teenager, looking for a few extra dollars. But not enough to feed a family of one adult, two kids, and a baby. Mom was no longer a teen, but she stretched that money as far as she could. For years, it was our household's sole income.

We lived in the country, about an hour-and-a-half drive from Pittsburgh. It was the early '60s, when newspapers published a morning and an evening edition each weekday, and one in the morning only on Saturday and Sunday. And we delivered them. On foot. In weather fair and foul. School or no school.

My brother and I would get up at five in the morning and deliver in the dark. There weren't many streetlights out there, but there were plenty of dogs. Some would bite you if you did not approach them in the right way. Fortunately, our family dog walked along with me as I threw papers.

Even now, when winter's on the wind—or if the day is just cold and rainy, chilling me to the bone—it reminds me. Because that's how it was for us as kids, all winter long. My mother didn't seem to care if we had gloves or coats. We were just kids, doing what she told us and fending for ourselves.

Something else I remember is the day my dog got hit by a car. I had to cross a busy road to take the paper to one house. It was a major highway, and a car hit him. He was a mixed-breed German shepherd, pretty much the same size as me. I carried him for what had to be a mile, as my five-year-old brain comprehended it, back to our house. He was bleeding from the mouth, and I woke my mother.

I remember telling her, "Mom! We have to get the dog to the hospital! He's going to die!"

Her angry response when she woke up was, "Forget it, I don't have any money for that dog." I cried my eyes out as I watched my dog die. Even now I feel the painful sorrow as I remember this and write about it.

If only we had some money, I thought, *we could have saved that dog.*

* * *

Taking papers and then having to collect the money weekly from the customers on the route taught me a lot. I got to know my customers. I think because the town was so small, many knew that my father had left us and allowed me to do extra jobs to make more money. Several paid me to take their trash cans to the curb on trash pickup day, and I regularly shoveled the snow off of customers' sidewalks during my morning route. (Snow days meant getting up an hour earlier, at four instead of five in the morning.)

The money from these chores helped compensate for those few customers who would not answer the door when I came to collect payment for their newspapers. Because I was responsible for covering the cost of the papers when a customer did not pay, I would often go back to their houses multiple times to collect. Each time, I'd leave a handwritten note asking that they leave the money owed in an envelope on the doorstep for me to pick up when I delivered the next morning's newspaper. After three notices, I'd cut off their newspaper delivery. These were the same people who later called the newspaper office to complain about me.

My biggest lesson came when one of my customers asked if I had any silver quarters in my collection bag. (Quarters minted prior to 1965 were 90 percent silver.) I said that I did not know. He asked if it was OK if he looked at my coins. I thought he was a nice older gentleman and naively allowed him to pour my collection bag of coins onto his kitchen counter. He promised to give me an equal amount of other coins or dollar bills in exchange for any silver ones he found.

I had no idea—until the next day, when my mother counted the money before taking it to the *Herald Standard* office—that I was short. Turned out this "gentleman" was a thief, and it took me weeks of extra jobs to make it up. But it was a valuable lesson that I've never forgotten: people are not always who they seem to be.

Figuring it out

Though we qualified, my mother was too proud to go on welfare. When she finally realized my dad was never coming back, she decided to apply for food stamps. But Mom was embarrassed to use them herself, plus our car was old and never worked. So she sent *me*, at six-and-a-half, on a bus to the grocery store. It ran a loop between Hopwood (where I lived) and Uniontown.

I'd get on the bus with a limited number of food stamps and a grocery list put together with my brother's help (remember, we were the family cooks). I had to pick out the groceries (knowing I could only carry two bags), calculate in my head how much I was spending (I could not go over the amount I had in food stamps), and check out before the bus came back.

As stressful as this was on a little kid, what was worse was the shame I felt when I pulled out the food stamps to pay for the groceries. I was embarrassed by our need for them, too, and feared that a kid from my grade-school class would see me.

Looking back, I think again: *If only we had money …*

* * *

If my mother had actually gone in for a diagnosis, I think she would have been considered bipolar. She had some real highs, but mostly lows. My mom's mother blamed it on an incident from Mom's childhood.

Workmen were repairing the roof of Mom's school, and she happened to be in the wrong place—three stories below—at the wrong time. A crowbar fell from above, catching my mom square on the head. Grandmother said she was in a coma for days, and when she awoke, she was a very different and moody kid. I know this story is true because there is a very large scar on my mother's scalp that is evident when her hair is wet.

Her moodiness manifested regularly when we were kids. One day, I came home from school to find that Mom had painted the walls in our living room a dark blue. She'd also moved a large mirror from the entryway, which had given our tiny house the illusion of more depth. She said she was tired of seeing her "fat self" in that mirror. It was the start of a very dark period for her, and it lasted a long time.

Maybe you're stunned that we had a house at all, and I don't blame you. It was thanks entirely to the generosity of my grandfather on my dad's side. Even though he did not like my father and never believed my father was actually his son—he'd spent just one night with my father's mother, upon his return from the Navy—fortunately for us, he loved my brother the moment he met him. He loved me, too.

This grandpa was a successful builder who made a lot of money building houses on land purchased with my Grandmother Ann's savings, earned while she was working as a bookkeeper for a prominent local business. Grandmother Ann never had children and loved her job. When my brother and I were toddlers, Grandpa built a modest three-bedroom ranch house in an actual subdivision for us to live in. It was clean and neat, but our paper routes were not enough to pay the bills after our father left.

Growing up without money in Hopwood was tough. Despite having a nice little house in a nice neighborhood, our water, gas, and electricity were regularly shut off.

My mother's solution—for water, at least—was to send us out before getting the morning papers, when it was still dark and the neighbors were still sleeping. We'd use their hoses to fill buckets of water and wrestle them to our bathtub, to have water that day.

Many times, I wished we lived in a neighborhood like the one where my mother's parents lived, where everyone was poor. It was embarrassing to wear my brother's hand-me-downs when I was not a boy and my girlfriends were wearing nice skirts and pretty dresses. It was hard to act like I was not hungry, because I could not afford to eat in the school cafeteria with my friends. It was hard to keep finding reasons why my friends could not come to my house, as I was too ashamed to have them see our beat-up furniture or to find that our utilities had been turned off.

Looking back on these hard times in my life, I know they made me who I am today.

I also thank God that my mom did not just give up and put us all up for adoption. It was not easy for her. I can only imagine the pain and heartache she went through as she raised us alone, without the help of our father. I will be forever grateful to her for this sacrifice.

* * *

Early in this chapter, I asked a question: Why do people seek my help in protecting and growing their wealth?

I hope the story of my early life makes the answer obvious: because I don't want anyone, upon reaching retirement, to wonder—like I did as a child—what *could* have been "if only we had money."

I've lived the pain that a lack of money brings. The experience fuels my determination to do all I can to keep my clients from ever knowing that pain and to encourage proper estate planning that leaves a legacy to those they love.

> I've lived the pain that a lack of money brings. The experience fuels my determination to do all I can to keep my clients from ever knowing that pain.

Above and beyond

I learned from my paper route days that if you give your customers more than they expect, they love you. As I got older, I began thinking like an entrepreneur.

I'd clean a couple of our neighbors' houses regularly and babysit others' kids. Once the kids were in bed, I'd clean the house, too, and get a big tip. It all went to supporting the family, but that spirit—of just figuring things out, doing what you have to do—never leaves you.

It also steels one's resolve. I was still young, but this much I knew: *I would escape poverty.*

I knew very early that I wanted to be a physician. That wonderful grandfather who built our house died when I was young, maybe seven years old. We loved him; he was just the greatest. He was also wealthy, and while he wouldn't support us (beyond *building that house!*) he had horses, and we'd go and ride.

He died of leukemia. I remember him getting blood transfusions in Pittsburgh and coming back with energy again. Later, I thought,

"If I were a doctor, I could have saved him." Not even knowing, of course, because leukemia is leukemia. Still, losing him so young really piqued my interest in becoming a doctor.

Something else did too. I had pretty severe eczema wherever my skin touched skin: inside my elbow, the back of my legs. The itching was unbearable. When our water was on, I'd run it as hot as possible from the faucet and let it run on the affected areas, just to kill the pain.

We didn't have money for doctors, so I didn't know what it was. When I went off to college, the medical facility diagnosed it and gave me cortisone cream. To me, it was a miracle drug!

During high school, I volunteered at the Uniontown hospital as a candy striper. Because I wanted to be a doctor, I wanted to see what it was like to work in a hospital. I volunteered as often as possible, but never missed a Sunday. I ended up putting in so many hours that the hospital gave me an award. It looked great on my med school application, but I wasn't putting in hours to get recognition. I wanted to help people.

When I commit to something, I fully immerse myself in it, and later, during my undergrad studies, I committed completely to a future in medicine. I'd already applied to med school, and planned on going to Philly, when I met my future husband, Ken. It happened in physics class, in my final year at Pennsylvania State University.

Ken wanted to be a dentist. He'd narrowed it down to Boston, Pittsburgh, or Georgetown. He also wanted to get married. I believe he was afraid I would meet someone else in medical school, since back then, only a small percentage of med school students were women.

I had visited Boston when my brother and I visited a friend who was attending the New England Conservatory, and loved it. "If you go to Boston," I told Ken, "I'll marry you and apply to medical schools up there."

So here we were, two newlywed, soon-to-be medical professionals. It would be another year before I could join a new school cohort, and I wanted to put that year to the best possible use. I figured as a dentist and a medical doctor we'd have money someday, and that I should know what to do with it. So I decided to learn firsthand.

It was a choice that changed my life forever.

CHAPTER 2

My Planning Meets Reality!

I'VE MENTIONED MY BOTTOM-LINE mentality. There's no doubt my impoverished youth contributed to it, but my innate curiosity factored in as well. It fueled an unlikely partnership that foretold my future, though I never suspected it at the time.

I had a teenage friend whose grandfather loved reading the *Wall Street Journal,* writing down his stocks' current valuations, and figuring out his dividend income. My friend had no interest in what his grandfather was doing, but I found it fascinating and, when visiting his house, spent more time with his grandfather than with my friend.

His grandfather spent hours talking to me about his stocks in railroads and utilities. He'd show me the current price, what he paid for it, and the amount the company paid out quarterly in dividends. Of the many things he taught me, one piece of advice has stayed with me all my life: "Investing in dividend-paying stocks is one of the smartest things to do with money." It had clearly worked for him, and he patiently explained to me how his investments paid him an income.

He said investing in stocks was better than owning real estate. He'd owned a small apartment building and found it to be a pain when tenants had problems to show up and fix them. He was a lot happier collecting his stock dividends and not getting phone calls from renters in the middle of the night.

I remembered his tutelage when Ken and I arrived in Boston, and decided that if I worked at a brokerage firm while Ken went to dental school, I'd learn all about what my friend's grandfather was doing—and I was excited!

Shearson

I took a job as a sales assistant at Shearson's retail brokerage office in Chestnut Hill. Within a very short time I knew which brokers— as they were known back in the day—were respected and loved by their clients, who did a good job and who was getting complaints. I approached whom I considered the smartest stock guy and the best bond guy with a proposal.

"If you'll give me a little time at the end of every day and answer my questions and explain investments to me, I'll help you out in return," I said. "After work, I'll post your books [at the time, all brokers had to keep handwritten records of all of their buy/sell transactions] and type letters for you." I couldn't type very well, but with a lot of effort—and Wite-Out—I got it done accurately.

Both guys took me up on it. To say I learned a lot is an understatement.

Danny was the stock guy. He would allow me to borrow his books and his tapes—cassettes, to be precise. (I *told* you this was back in the day!) Through access to Danny's great library, I studied

Richard Wyckoff's theories on market cycles, pricing, and charting, which taught me about technical analysis. Danny also loaned me a book, *Security Analysis,* by Benjamin Graham and David Dodd, which detailed fundamental analysis.

Danny preferred lending me resources like these to explaining things in detail, but once in a while I'd ask, "Why were you buying this stock today?" or "What made that stock drop?" and he'd fill me in.

Percy, the bond guy, spent more time with me. His wife had recently died, and he would always answer my questions over dinner at the local Chinese restaurant or at Legal Sea Foods in Chestnut Hill. (My husband loved it: I was always sure to eat only half my meal and bring the other half home to him—a big treat, as we did not have extra money for dinners out.)

Percy hated the stock market. It had devastated his family during the Great Depression, and he sold vacuum cleaners door-to-door to survive. He wouldn't touch stocks but loved the bond market, and taught me everything he knew.

It was a really diverse office, and we probably had thirty brokers, some specializing in stocks, some in bonds, some in unit trusts or mutual funds, and some in annuities and insurance-related products. Others still specialized in more risky investments like options or commodities.

The commodity brokers seemed to be the most stressed. One was a heavy smoker, especially on turbulent days in the commodity markets. Management had the commodity brokers inside a glass-walled office inside the general office. You'd walk past on those turbulent days and it'd be like those rooms you used to see in airport terminals, with glass doors, filled with smokers. I may not have known much about the business yet, but I knew that working as a commodity broker would never be for me!

The office also had options brokers. They would buy either "call" or "put" options on a stock to leverage their position, with one option contract equal to one hundred shares of the stock. Let me explain.

An option is an agreement between buyer and seller. It gives the right to the buyer and the obligation to the seller to buy or sell the stock prior to a specified date at a certain price. The person buying a call option is hoping the stock will rise in price. The one buying a put option wants the stock's price to drop. If the stock does not move above the specified price before the specified date (for the owner of the call option), or move below the specified price before the specified date (for the owner of the put option), the option's owner loses the money they've paid to secure the option.

I decided at the time that option trading was way too risky. It looked more like gambling than investing to me. Later in my career I was asked to become a registered options principal (ROP), and learned that options can actually be used to mitigate risk.[1]

Studying for the ROP exam—which I took primarily so I could sign off on option trades in the office—helped me understand market tools such as covered call writing, protected puts, and other strategies that few people in the general public had even heard of. I'd never be an options trader, but learning about options opened a door that I thought might help Ken and me invest wisely and later proved to be a valuable tool to assist me in serving my clients.

---

1   Options are not suitable for all investors. Typically, commissions are charged for options transactions. Transaction costs may be significant in multileg option strategies, including collars, as they involve multiple commission charges. Please contact your financial advisor for a copy of the Options Disclosure Document (ODD).

* * *

It's pretty uncommon for a sales assistant to dive in like I did. Back in the day, firms hired nice-looking girls for those jobs, and it seemed to me that most were single and hoping to find somebody.

I wasn't looking for anybody; I was married. I was there to learn, but also wanted to do a good job, because I learned as a kid that when you go above and beyond the job description, customers love it. So I did customer service to a T.

When a client called to talk to their broker about a dividend that had not been credited to their account, or did not understand why they were charged interest when they bought a bond, I'd step in to get the problem resolved. I'd ensure the dividend was applied or explain that the extra interest charge was accrued interest. Mundane stuff to me, but clients cared about it—and I knew that doing customer service well was critical to client loyalty.

I quickly became the office problem-solver. Other sales assistants and their brokers would ask me for help. "Just let me talk to the client," I'd say, and get things squared away.

I was a sponge, soaking up everything I could in the short year I'd *planned* on being there.

Then, reality came calling.

An unexpected promotion

About four months in, our office's operations manager died in an accident.

The office manager came to me and asked if I would step in and take over the job while he found a replacement. I told him I would only do so if he paid me an operations manager's salary, not my sales assistant salary. He agreed, and my salary was doubled.

We were so poor, with Ken in dental school and me a sales assistant. We were eating a lot of mac and cheese, never going out or anything. We'd have maybe seven dollars left at the end of the week, which we would use on Friday night to buy a greasy pizza and a couple of cheap, headache-inducing beers. Ken was overjoyed when I came home with the news of this promotion, even though I expected it to be short term. My plans were still to go to medical school.

On my first day as the office operations manager, I saw there was no manual, no set procedures, no systems in place. Everything was being done seat-of-the-pants. So that was job number one: I wrote a manual that spelled everything out, including how to enter wire orders onto the various trading floors and how to handle trade errors when they happened. I put in place set procedures for taking in checks, cash, stock certificates, and bearer bonds.

A big concern was the handling of the cash, but the biggest was stewardship of bearer municipal bonds. These had no names on them, unlike stock certificates, which have the name of the owner typed on the front of the certificate. They behave like cash but carry ridiculous face values. If somebody stole one, they'd just stolen twenty-five grand, or whatever its value was. That never happened on my watch, but before I got the ops job it could have—so I did something else immediately: put operations in a locking cage. No one got in without my say-so.

I was a tough manager!

Full commitment

But I still had a lot to learn. For example, an old rule of sales management, known as the 80/20 rule, states that 80 percent of a company's sales come from 20 percent of its salesforce.

As ops manager, I saw every trade in the branch, and found that the 80/20 rule was absolutely true, as 80 percent of the office's gross production came from 20 percent of the brokers. I also discovered a corollary: the 80 percent of the sales staff that wasn't producing much took up 80 percent of the operations staff's time, solving problems that were, many times, created by those brokers. The group was notorious for filling out new account paperwork incorrectly, for having stock certificates signed in the wrong place, and for making trade errors. Apparently, from lack of practice.

In a financial setting, bad paperwork is a real time drain.

"Get rid of that 80 percent," I told my boss, "and we won't have all these errors to correct."

He wouldn't do it—which, I'd also learn, was right in step with the times. The extended bull market meant companies could afford to keep the hangers-on, low sales, paperwork mistakes, trade errors, and all.

Still, I was running my operations department pretty lean. We had two full-timers besides myself—a cashier and a wire operator—but I used college interns for most everything else, to keep costs down.

Soon after the firm hired a new advisor trainee, however, I got the lesson that would ultimately transform my med school planning to a whole new reality.

When he gave his first paycheck to my cashier for deposit into his account, I saw that he—a broker trainee!—was making *two times* what I was, running the place! I went straight to the boss to find out why. My manager responded quite matter-of-factly: "That's what Shearson pays trainees."

As a sales assistant, I had already learned about the best bonds to buy, what stocks you look at, commodities, options, you name it. I'd taken the initiative to learn while earning a tiny fraction of what he was being paid. In fact, I was one of the people *training him!*

What's more, I'd already been thinking about staying another year. The work was interesting, and I'd doubled my salary in a few short months. By working another year, Ken and I could save some money for his last year at Tufts Dental School—enough to carry us both while I undertook my first year of med school.

Seeing that trainee's check, however, really crystalized things. We could be setting a lot more aside, and I decided: it was time to get paid for my hard work! I went to the manager to tell him that I wanted in the training program.

"I can't let you go into the broker training program," my boss told me. "We need you as operations manager."

"OK," I said, not missing a beat.

"But I won't be in tomorrow. I'm going to see the E. F. Hutton manager down the street to ask to get into the Hutton training program. Or I'll go down to Dean Witter, or Merrill Lynch." All those brokerages were an easy commute from my Jamaica Plain apartment, and they all had training programs.

He gave in, but made me pay my own way to fly to Shearson's New York headquarters and interview with the head of the training program, in hopes, I guess, that I'd change my mind.

I flew to New York. I'm sure my boss figured they'd turn me down, because the training program department head was known to be tough—plus, they wanted salespeople, folks who could handle rejection. The popular wisdom was that people on the ops side couldn't take it.

Little did they know.

I was used to rejection. I got plenty of it as a kid, mostly thanks to my mom. Besides being blamed for the varicose veins that came during her pregnancy with me, she also made it clear to me that I was stupid, not pretty, and a mistake, as she wanted another boy. I never remember my mom ever hugging me or saying she loved me, yet I saw her do this plenty of times with my brother, Bruce.

My mom, who was beautiful as a young woman, loved to watch the Miss America and Miss Universe pageants every year, and to assess every girl. "Her ears are too big," or, "Her legs are too skinny." And these were the most beautiful women in the world! I'd be sitting there on the floor, this little girl, thinking, "Oh my God. I must be so ugly." There was nothing I could do about my looks, but there was plenty I could do to prove that I was not stupid. Maybe this was part of my drive for success.

As it goes, the head of the Shearson training program interviewed me, and, I like to think, recognized my drive. Rightly so. For someone who grew up in my home environment, a rejected sales pitch was mere child's play.

I got in, and the program was state of the art. We stayed in beautiful condos behind the Dow Jones building and walked to the twin towers for training on the 102nd floor. There were thirty-six in our cohort; I was one of four women.

It was demanding, but I loved it. They covered *everything*. Stocks, bonds, commodities, options, unit trusts, mutual funds. And every *sector*. Shearson brought in analysts at the top of their respective games who taught us to think critically, asking questions like "Why you'd do this, instead of that?"

Danny and Percy had given me a great foundation. I understood the basics of investing. Thanks to my ROP studies, I knew how to buy a stock and hedge against downside risks. But in the training program, we learned how to read a balance sheet and how events drive the markets. All of it in great depth. Plus, we could pick and choose what interested us, and each of us did. This training program set the foundation for my bottom-line approach: a dedication to helping clients get as much appreciation on their money as possible while keeping risk to a minimum.

* * *

Upon completing training and getting back to the office, you were expected to put what you'd learned to use right away—by selling. So we were assigned the hardest kind of selling there is: cold calling. This meant experiencing rejection, and plenty of it.

Other trainees' managers would buy them prospect lists. Not mine, even though he had paid for cold-calling lists for other trainees in my branch office. (Was he still hoping I'd focus on ops? Probably.)

No matter. I created my own.

It happened thanks to one of the guys in our office, who I knew had graduated from Harvard. I asked to borrow his university directory. It had contact info for people in every graduating class, and when Harvard came out with a new bond to fund this or that project, I'd call alumni whose year of graduation indicated they should be in retirement at the time of my cold call.

But municipal bonds—munis—formed the foundation of my future. I figured that muni bond buyers were wealthy enough to have a tax problem. (Due to their higher income, they want to own muni bonds because the interest is nontaxable.) Wealthy clients were what I needed, so I decided to build my foundation of clients with muni bond investors.[2]

---

2   Municipal bonds are federally tax-free but may be subject to state and local taxes, and interest income may be subject to federal alternative minimum tax (AMT). Bonds are subject to availability and market conditions; some have call features that may affect income. Bond prices and yields are

Another way I would identify prospective bond buyers was by driving through wealthy neighborhoods and noting the addresses of the most expensive houses. Then it was off to the library, which, back then, had directories from which you could cross-reference names from addresses. With those two pieces of info, I could often get a phone number from directory assistance, because everyone still had land lines.

Being a woman helped in cold calling, especially if your voice sounded like a twelve-year-old, as did mine. The wife would usually answer my call. I'd introduce myself, ask for her husband—and then, I'd hear something like this.

"Honey, there's a little girl on the phone wanting to talk to you. She's probably going to try to sell you Girl Scout cookies."

I'd hear him pick up the extension.

"Hello?"

"Hi," I'd say. "I've got this great Harvard bond," or if they lived in Brookline, "Brookline is coming out with a new muni bond issue."

"*What?*"

"Yeah, hi. I'm Debra Brede with Shearson."

I'd get them talking, and we'd have the *best* conversations!

When we'd finally meet, these guys would always say, "You know—you sound like a kid on the phone!"

That was fine with me. I parlayed my twelve-year-old voice and cold-call lists into a base of clients. But doing just bonds was—ugh. Like watching paint dry.

I loved to study the stock market and found stocks to be a lot more interesting. The more I read about various companies—what they were doing, the excitement of it, the growth opportunities—the

---

inversely related: when the price goes up, the yield goes down, and vice versa. Market risk is a consideration if sold or redeemed prior to maturity.

harder I'd work on getting my bond clients into stocks. But many resisted, based on fear of losing that money.

So I steered them around it.

I noticed they weren't spending their interest income, and that many times when their bonds came due they'd just roll them over into another muni. So, when their interest income built up to a certain amount in their money market accounts, I would call and recommend a good dividend-paying stock (taking a page out of my childhood friend's grandfather's book). I would often pick a strong electric utility, or a "blue-chip" stock: a household name sort of company whose products the client would be familiar with.

Some clients were *still* wary of risk. That's where my ROP training came in.

"We'll buy a put, to protect you from the downside," I'd explain. "This way, we'll just have to monitor the spread and cover the cost of the put, which we can do with some of the stock's dividend income."

This was back in '85. Little did I know we would have a bull market that lasted the rest of the '80s and throughout the '90s. I was selling the way I wanted to, by putting clients' interests first, and it's how I've worked ever since.

I've never wanted to be like one broker in our office—I'll call him Aaron—who would have angry clients *accost him on the street.*

We'd go down to the corner store to get something for lunch, and Aaron would say, "We can't go down that aisle; that guy right there hates me." But we'd run into the guy at the checkout, or an entirely different client on the walk back, and he'd jump all over Aaron. It was tough to watch.

Aaron loved buying speculative stocks, mainly new issues, and going for the big payoff. He was a great salesman, personable and funny. But when those issues tanked, it wasn't Aaron who lost the principal he used to buy them; it was his clients.

So much for med school

My reality is a far cry from my original plan.

The financial industry spirited me away from a career in medicine. Instead of MD, today I've got AIF® behind my name (the Accredited Investment Fiduciary designation).

Nonetheless, I serve on the board of trustees and the finance committee of one of New England's leading healthcare institutions. I am also fortunate to serve on the Institutional Review Board/ Human Research Committee of Partners HealthCare, so I read lots of protocols for cutting-edge research, written in scientific terms so dense that I keep a medical dictionary handy. And I love every minute of it.

My point? Changing my career path never altered my love for medicine nor my commitment to helping others. It extends well beyond my clients, to local and regional helping institutions—and even to countries on the other side of the globe, as I'll soon share.

My hard-won success as an investment advisor has permitted me to follow through on that commitment, in ways I might not have been able to if I'd gone into medicine. That fact has only underlined, for me, the importance of keeping an open mind in all we do.

A childhood like mine brings the fragility of all life into sharp focus, from the family dog who followed me on my paper route to the beloved grandfather who quite literally put a roof over my head. I look back, and I remember how differently things *could* have turned out. But because I maintained an openness to possibility, and because people cared enough to help at key moments, things worked out.

I believe this drives us—that it must drive us, if we are successful and have any humanity at all—to help others. To see that we're all vulnerable, and to accept that we, one day, will join all those who have gone before us in whatever comes next.

What could be a more noble aim than helping those who are with us now to find their way?

CHAPTER 3

The Best Teacher

Experience is the teacher of all things.

—Julius Caesar

THE ABOVE QUOTE is probably more familiar to you in its modern-ized form: "Experience is the best teacher." We often hear it from people who have enjoyed long-term success in a particular field.

In my thirty-three years as an investment advisor, I have seen it all. Over the course of this book, I'll share key experiences that have shaped my approach to preserving and growing my clients' wealth in retirement.

But before one can *grow* wealth, they must establish and secure it. Time and again, I've seen people lose capital that could have produced wealth, thanks to their willingness to accept some dangerous assumptions. The most common, by far, is that whomever they entrust with their capital will invest it with their best interests in mind.

Remember Aaron, the broker I mentioned in chapter 2, who feared chance meetings with former (foaming-at-the-mouth) clients? Aaron put his customers' money in highly speculative stocks and quite often lost it. Like a ballplayer who wants desperately to be the hero, he constantly swung for the fence, when a single or a double would have been the smarter option. On rare occasions Aaron would hit a homer, and his client loved it. But more often than not he struck out, and most clients hated him for it.

That's understandable. But was it entirely Aaron's fault?

Investors who want to protect and grow wealth have an up-front responsibility: to be sure those advising them understand their long-term goals and appetite for risk.

The fiduciary standard

The AIF behind my name stands for Accredited Investment Fiduciary. Earning that designation took a lot of work, and it's one I'm proud of. Yet it's also one of those phrases that—let's face it—can make people's eyes glaze over.

That's too bad, because its meaning is actually quite simple. An AIF is trained—and *duty-bound*—to put his or her clients' *best interests* first.

Much is being said and written these days about "self-directed investing." It sounds terrific, right? "Take charge of your finances!" "Be responsible for your own wealth!"

But the reality is very different. Many people who have experienced great success in the business world are discovering that the logic that played a key role in that success doesn't always help in protecting and growing their wealth. That's because good *investment* decisions rest not only on logic, but also on understanding behavioral finance—the reasons why rational people can often make irrational decisions when it comes to money and investing.

In other words, it is not enough to identify a company with good management, quality products, good growth prospects, and strong earnings. Good investment decisions require having the discipline *not* to react to the behavior of the crowd—whether it is caught up in greed (for example, buying overvalued tech stocks in late 1999/ early 2000) or in fear (like selling out during market downturns).

It's the oldest axiom on Wall Street: buy low, sell high. But for people not trained in doing so, it is much (much!) easier said than done.

A seasoned advisor who upholds the fiduciary standard and understands the markets' ins and outs can spot at five hundred yards faulty assumptions and approaches—the potential pitfalls of moves which seem perfectly rational to people whose lifelong priority has been to avoid losing their companies' money.

"Danny, buying opportunity"

When I joined Shearson as a sales assistant in the '80s, hoping simply to learn about investing during my year before med school, I quickly saw which brokers put their clients first. Needless to say, Aaron was not one of them.

As noted in chapter 2, I gravitated instead to Danny (and Percy). I had no inkling that I'd become a broker. But I imagined that if I did, I'd want my clients to love me. When it came to stocks, Danny was the broker every client seemed to love, so I wanted to know why.

Danny gave me cassette tapes and books while I was a sales assistant, but they only hinted at the answer. They featured some of the most successful market gurus of the day and covered a lot of fundamentals, but didn't tell me exactly *what* Danny did, and *why*. But when world events sent Shearson's squawk boxes into orbit, I got my answer.

In April of 1986, when the Chernobyl nuclear power plant blew, I was still a relatively new broker. The squawk box went crazy. (A squawk box was an intercom speaker that allowed a firm's analysts and traders to communicate with the firm's brokers. The digital age made them obsolete.) Electric utility stocks were getting pounded, phones were ringing off their hooks, and clients were scared as they watched those issues drop in price.

Brokers knew they could make two trades and get commissions on both: the sale of the utility stock and the purchase of a replacement stock in a different industry or sector of the market.

But Danny was my mentor, and thanks to his months of tutelage, my instincts (and his) took over. My desk was right across from Danny's office. I looked at him and said, "Danny, buying opportunity." He smiled and nodded, "Yeah, buying opportunity."

We called our clients and told them to buy more electric utilities, even as some of the other brokers were selling their clients out of utilities into something else and doubling their commissions. In Danny's view as well as mine, they were doing their clients a disservice.

If you put the clients first, it wasn't just any buying opportunity, it was a great one. All electric utilities were plummeting—even those *not* invested in nuclear. We knew those stocks would rebound as investors connected the dots and realized that people depend on electricity and that electric utilities were needed to provide it.

I'd learned a long time ago that it is always best not to panic but instead to assess the situation and react appropriately. In other words, it made sense that electric utilities that use nuclear to power their plants would drop after the Chernobyl nuclear power plant accident. But was it logical to see electric utilities that only used coal, natural gas, or petroleum to power their plants also drop in value? The answer was "No!"

Some of the other brokers flat out took advantage of the situation, reinforcing the fears that were driving the drop in the electric utility sector of the stock market. Selling out electric utility stocks after the news of the accident at Chernobyl meant they were selling low, not high—as that old axiom urges. By acting on their clients' fears, they hurt their clients' investment returns. These same brokers should have explained that unexpected events happen, and that stocks in good companies will often rebound from the initial short-term hit.

It is also important to understand that markets are cyclical. (I'll talk more about this in chapter 6.)

Years later I'd see the same thing, with the Deepwater Horizon blowout and massive oil spill in the Gulf of Mexico. British Petroleum (BP) wasn't the only energy stock that got hit. Companies not doing deepwater drilling did too. So again, buying opportunity. Some of the top active mutual fund managers did just that: they identified these companies dropping in the heat of the moment, bought them, and were rewarded as these companies' stock prices rebounded.

Doing what is best for my clients means being a voice of reason in the midst of a market sector meltdown, helping my clients not to act in fear but instead to take advantage of the opportunities that unexpected events and changes in market cycles bring. It also means putting in the extra work needed to keep my clients' portfolios diversified so as to help protect them during unexpected corrections.

When is a blue-chip not a blue-chip?

I learned a lot from my mentor, Danny. He bought really good stocks that paid good dividends for his clients. He totally avoided the speculative stuff, like options and commodities. He just bought blue chips.

But even stocks widely regarded as blue-chip issues can be dangerous.

In 1999, a client's friend came to see me. She worked in the management echelons at General Electric and was retiring in a few months. At the time of our meeting, she had all of her investable assets in GE stock. Many corporate leaders make the mistake of investing their savings almost exclusively in their company's stock. It's especially true at large organizations with storied histories that, like GE, have successfully diversified the company into smaller sub-companies within the parent organization. GE was known to have multiple business lines that could service many sectors of the global economy.

The wide range of markets large companies serve is often at the heart of their leaders' tendency to put all their eggs in the one corporate basket. It certainly was in her case, as we will soon see.

Frontline workers in such organizations often do the same thing. They buy company stock for their 401(k)s, thinking they are killing two birds with one stone: they are not only supporting their employer but are also making a safe investment in a company they feel they know firsthand.

Company leaders might feel the same way, but the sense that they are supporting the company—in particular the message that doing so sends to the markets—is probably the bigger factor. If they don't have enough faith in their own organization to put significant skin in the game, after all, why would independent investors do it?

Whatever the reasoning, both groups are dead wrong. Putting all your eggs in one basket is foolish, even if the company you work for is diversified, with many different products and services in many different sectors of the economy. Why? Because it is still *one* company, with *one* executive management team and *one* board of directors steering its direction.

Unfortunately, my prospective client ignored my best efforts to tell her so.

General Electric stock began a steady climb in the mid-'90s, topping out in August 2000 at $58.17 a share—a more than threefold increase in just over three-and-a-half years. But the majority of company profits were coming from its financial services side and the jet engine business. It took only the failure of the financial services business for the stock to plummet.

For 111 years, GE was one of the select companies whose performance was gauged by the Dow Jones Industrial Average. It was, by definition, a blue-chip stock. Yet in June of 2018, the Dow removed it. As I write, GE stock sits at less than 25 percent of its August 2000 high, and some are wondering if the company will survive.

And that prospective client who sat down with me years ago? She did not hire me, as she did not like my recommendation to diversify her investment portfolio. In 2010, the client who originally referred this GE retiree to me mentioned in our review meeting that her friend sold out all her GE stock the prior year, at around six dollars per share. She could not take it anymore and was afraid she would lose everything. It saddened me. This prospective client remained convinced that GE's many businesses assured its long-term prosperity. She kept the shares upon retirement and paid the price: she's back working at a job and for a wage that pale in comparison to her heady days at GE.

Reading that story, you might think, *GE was a unique situation. The odds of it happening again are slim to none.* I'm here to say that's 100 percent wrong. Companies have been and are continuing to buy each other at a dizzying pace. As corporate consolidation continues, the odds of another GE debacle only increase. But the bigger point is this: if you put all your eggs in one basket, you expose them all to breaking.

GE—the company—was diversified. But it was not balanced. Its investments in the industries it served varied wildly. Its revenues from businesses beyond jet engines and financial services were scant by comparison, among those that were profitable at all.

A knowledgeable wealth advisor will look to ensure their clients' portfolios are not exposed to excess risk because of owning a concentrated position in one stock. I believe true diversification of investments means not putting more than 5 percent of your money in any one issue. I don't care what company it is, or how blue that blue-chip stock is perceived to be.

By starting with that mind-set, and with careful and continuous analysis of a client's portfolio, a good advisor can help save their clients from devastating losses (resulting from owning a concentrated stock position) when a bad earnings report and analysts' downgrade come and the once-beloved stock drops suddenly.

It's a reality too many GE shareholders—including employees—learned the hard way. One hundred and eleven years as a blue-chip issue is an awfully good run. But nothing lasts forever. Without an objective advisor keeping an eye on the fundamentals, you're far more likely to have too much of your money in the wrong place at the wrong time.

Other fundamentals matter too

When I broke into investing, you seldom heard about retirement planning, and "wealth management" was a phrase not yet coined. My training was broad and deep, but the big brokerage houses put their people through it for one reason only: to increase sales.

My approach to building my client base—cold calling muni bond investors, buying bonds for them, and then gradually buying blue-chip, dividend-paying stocks and using put options to protect from downside risk—might seem inventive. But invention's mother, necessity, is what really drove it: my prospects' first priority was *protecting* their wealth, not growing it. Otherwise, they wouldn't have been in bonds in the first place.

Their concerns, combined with wanting my clients to love the job I do for them, are what charted the course of my career, long before wealth management became a thing. I knew it was what I wanted to do, there was just no name for it. Yet.

Because I saw the importance of estate planning for wealthy clients, I started offering seminars in it, renting venues and bringing in estate planning attorneys. Despite their wealth, many of the prospective clients didn't have proper estate plans.

Instead, most couples had pretty much everything in joint accounts. That seems fine on its face, and for most of the population it often is. When one partner dies, the account goes in full to the surviving spouse. Simple.

But for wealthy people, proper titling of assets was a key factor in protecting their wealth from unnecessary tax liability—as I saw firsthand in 1989 with a client I'll call Evelyn.

Evelyn came to me through an existing client soon after her husband, Richard, died. At our first meeting, she gave me copies of her statements from a well-known brokerage firm showing her investment holdings. She had a little over $1 million in a nonretirement account titled in her name. I asked if there were any investment assets in her deceased husband's name. Evelyn said this brokerage account, now in her name, had been in joint name with her husband. It had been set up with rights of survivorship while her husband was alive, meaning everything belonged to the survivor once one of them died.

I asked if she and Richard had ever done any estate planning. Evelyn said an in-law, an estate planning attorney, had executed trust documents several years ago for her and her husband. Perhaps the attorney had failed to explain clearly that it was best to split in half their nonretirement investment assets and move them into two new accounts in the name of their new revocable trusts. Perhaps Evelyn and her husband did not understand that they needed to do it.

Whichever was true, Evelyn only learned after Richard's death that her investments were not titled in the most tax-advantageous way. With everything in their brokerage account titled with rights of survivorship, she suddenly had $1 million—and the estate tax liability it would carry, upon *her* death.

At the time, you could exempt $600,000 from federal estate taxes upon the owner's death. If they had split the assets, with $500,000 titled to each of their revocable trusts, there would be no federal estate taxes due upon their deaths. But if Evelyn died now, the amount of her estate in excess of $600,000 would be subject to estate tax of 55 percent. The remaining $400,000 would create a tax bill of $220,000—simply because Evelyn and her late husband hadn't titled their holdings correctly!

If they had done so prior to Richard's death, his share ($500,000) would have been below the exemption limit, and their daughter would have kept everything. It was merely a matter of doing the *paperwork* right. But they hadn't.

* * *

Many married couples have joint accounts with rights of survivorship that were *set up* with capital well below the federal estate tax exemption limit (known as the unified credit), but the capital *appreciates* enough over time to exceed it. It's an easy-to-overlook detail, a problem waiting to happen—especially for those trying to self-manage their financial planning. But when one spouse dies, the IRS will *not* overlook it. That's what happened in Evelyn's case, and when it does, there are limited options for making the situation better.

Gifting is one. Evelyn could have started giving her daughter the money. The maximum tax-free gift one could give another person at the time was $10,000 per year, so in 40 years ... but Evelyn was seventy-five! And of course, the account could *continue* to appreciate, if Evelyn did not need all the income and growth generated on the investments she owned.

She could hope the estate tax exemption would change. In fact, it did increase to $1 million in 2002, in what would have been Evelyn's favor—had she not died years before. Steee-rike two.

In the end, I advised Evelyn to cover her daughter's future tax liability with a life insurance policy. When Evelyn died, her daughter would use the death benefit funds to pay the estate taxes owed to the IRS. I'm not a fan of whole life insurance in general, but in this case, it was the best option among several bad ones.

What's saddest about this story is that a good wealth advisor would have caught it. But Evelyn and her late husband had no such professional looking over their holdings on anything like a regular basis.

The brother-in-law/estate planning attorney set up the trust, but none of their trusted advisors noticed that their assets were not titled in a way to allow them to make use of the $600,000 federal estate tax exemption. They had their investments held at a well-known brokerage firm, but the financial advisor must not have been knowledgeable on basic estate planning. Remember, financial advisors cannot give legal or tax advice, but there are no security regulations that keep a financial advisor from referring a client to an estate attorney or an accountant. That means the financial advisor needs to know enough on the subject of estate planning or tax planning to know when he or she needs to make that referral. But this basic and simple proper titling of assets never happened for Evelyn and it wound up costing her—in the form of unexpected insurance premiums.

Again, this was back in the late '80s. But throughout my career, I've advised clients whose joint assets exceed the exemption limit to meet with an estate planning attorney and, upon execution of the trusts, to send a copy to me, so my office can retitle their assets accordingly. Indeed, it becomes my top priority, because they're just one tragedy away from needlessly wiping out much of their estates through unnecessary taxation.

* * *

I also see faulty beneficiary titling in retirement accounts. It's especially common with second marriages, and typically goes like this.

The holder of a retirement account (be it a traditional IRA or 401(k), a Roth version, a profit-sharing plan, pension, or whatever) who has remarried wants to ensure that the account's assets ultimately go to his children. He assumes he will die first, as the percentages show that women typically outlive men. He wants to take care of the income needs of his second wife, but his primary goal is getting those assets to his kids (assuming she survives him) after she has died.

Without sound estate planning advice, many in this situation will list the new spouse as their retirement account's primary beneficiary and their children as contingent beneficiaries. Unfortunately, this ensures only that the assets are moved into a new IRA for the second spouse. Unless she names her deceased husband's children as the primary beneficiaries on this new IRA, her late husband's children *will not get the inheritance their father wanted them to have.*

Even if she lists her stepchildren as primary beneficiaries initially, when the new IRA is opened, it still doesn't guarantee they'll get those assets, because she is free to *change the beneficiaries* at any time. On more than one occasion, I've seen the stepmother remarry—and *change* the primary beneficiary *to her new spouse.* Sadly, it's not as rare as many people like to believe.

If the husband in our example had instead established a trust and named the trust as beneficiary of his retirement accounts, he could have stipulated that the trustee distribute all required minimum distributions (RMDs) to his second wife, along with any additional money needed to cover medical expenses or other needs he chose to provide for her. Most importantly, he could also have stipulated that all remaining assets go to his children after the death of his second wife. This would prevent his second wife from excluding her stepchildren as beneficiaries upon her death.

During the seminars I hosted all those years ago, I learned about many more problem situations that result from poor estate planning. It has helped me better serve my clients, right up to today. I'm not an attorney and cannot give legal advice; I'm not an accountant and can't give tax advice. But those sessions sharpened my sense of when something's not right and when to refer my client back to their attorney or accountant to ask the right questions.

If the client is not working with an estate attorney or accountant, I point them in a good direction. Over the years, I've vetted top-level attorneys and accountants who work at a fair price—resources I've used even for my own estate planning and accounting—and regularly recommend them to clients.

If they only knew

Though incorrect titling of assets can be damaging if not caught in time, it's one of the easier things to correct. Much more difficult is client close-mindedness.

Its most dangerous manifestation, by far, is when people convince themselves that something is *not* too good to be true, despite someone intimate with the industry—me, for example—warning them that it is. That's what happened with a referral that came to me in the mid-2000s.

This prospective client had $80 million dollars in investable assets, most of which was in municipal bonds that were spread over several brokerage firms. He'd been referred by a well-respected attorney who had seen municipal bond portfolios I had built for several of his law firm's clients.

So this new referral and his wife are sitting in my office, and I'm telling them about the top bond inventory available, including the current yields in the muni market, how I'd ladder their portfolio, and this and that. And the guy says, "Well, I am using a money manager I met down in Palm Beach and he has been getting 12 percent consistently for me."

Trying not to fall out of my chair, I said, "12 percent *consistently?*"

It just wasn't possible.

"Back in the early '80s," I said, "you could get those kinds of yields on munis because interest rates were so high. Maybe you're getting a 12 percent coupon? But in the current bond market, you're paying a premium for it, so your yield at maturity is not going to be 12 percent."

"No, no," he told me. "It's not in munis. I've got about $60 million in munis, but this other $20 million is with this other manager. Name is Madoff."

History tells us what happened next, but I'm making a larger point.

Here's a guy sitting on $80 million of investable assets. He's clearly no idiot. He's talking to someone, such as me, who is intimate with every available investment and their current yields. Yet he's *actually believing* that he's getting something nobody else is.

"Madoff," I say. "Sorry, I've never heard of him. What does he do?"

"Well, I don't know. I met him through somebody at the country club."

"Forgive me if I sound skeptical," I said. "In the current market, there is no safe investment that is consistently returning 12 percent. He might be in high-yield bonds, but they're risky. He could be doing it with option trading, using puts or calls, but that's risky too, and you're just not going to get 12 percent *consistently.* You might get 25 percent one year and lose money the next, but it's not going to just pay you 12 percent year in and year out."

But he was adamant.

"I don't know how he does it, but I get a 12 percent return every year, an even 12 percent. I used to have checks sent to me to fund our needs in retirement but now I am reinvesting this income."

"Well," I say, "let's just call him. Let's call him and ask what he's doing, and if it's better than coming to me for munis so be it, and you can just put more with him."

So this new prospective client gave me Madoff's direct number, and I was amazed when Madoff answered the phone. I introduced myself and then said, "I'm here with a client of yours and his wife."

He says, "Yeah?"

"Well," I say, "I'm just calling because they're asking my advice about putting more money with you."

"Well of course they should put it through me!" he says. "I do a great job for all of my clients."

"I understand you're getting a 12 percent return," I say. "But how are you getting that?"

And he says, "Why would I tell you?"

"I'm not trying to find out any of your secrets," I assured him. "I just want to know what the risk level is. Are you trading options? Are you buying high-yield bonds?"

"I don't talk about my investment strategies to anyone," he said. "If this client wants to put more money with me, he can put money with me. I have so many people that want me to invest for them that I turn away."

When the call ended, I said something I wouldn't typically say, something I'd never said to a client before.

"This guy's an ass. I wouldn't put a nickel with him, and I'd be pulling out anything he had of mine unless he told me how he's getting 12 percent."

Well, the wife, a very prim and proper lady—I saw her shoulders kind of go up. "I can't believe I just used the word ass!" I said to myself. But her husband sort of bailed me out.

"Well, I guess I won't put anything more with him, but I'm comfortable with what's happening now because I like that 12 percent return coming in."

We ended up buying munis for him and a nice mix of stocks; he became a client. But a few years later, in December of 2008, the news broke—and I get a call from his wife.

"Deb, did you hear the news about Bernie Madoff? What are we gonna do? How can we get our money?"

You hate to say, "Well, it's too late now," but that's what I had to say.

"Maybe you'll have some SIPC insurance, but I don't know what's going to happen with this whole thing since it was fraud."

SIPC (Security Investors Protection Corporation) insurance protects assets in a brokerage account, much like the FDIC protects assets in a bank. SIPC protects customers of SIPC-member broker-dealers if the firm fails financially. Coverage is up to $500,000 per customer for all accounts at the same institution, including a maximum of $250,000 for cash.

The problem for this client was that he had all of his $20 million in one account, registered in his name only. The picture was not pretty.

The exception that proves the rule

It's easy to write off the Bernie Madoff story as a rare example of greed run amok—both his own and that of his clients. To say, in hindsight, "How could they not know it was too good to be true?"

But looked at from a different perspective, it's the kind of cautionary tale each of us would do well to heed. After all, it's not surprising that a guy like Madoff—so brash and carelessly flaunting his ill-gained "success"—got caught. But how many other people calling themselves advisors are playing similar games, and doing a better job of concealing it?

I came up in the industry long before the Madoff scam but was seeing things I didn't like. They were a far cry from pyramid schemes, but to me, brokers putting their incomes ahead of their clients' best interests was just as bad, morally speaking. They'd double their incomes simply by selling clients out of one stock and into another stock, and sometimes for no good reason. Two transactions, two commissions, client after client.

> People were giving me their hard-earned money and trusting me to invest it wisely—it was as simple as that, and it still is.

I couldn't stomach that. I've *always* seen myself in a fiduciary role—and not just because it aligns with wanting my clients to love me. Even though financial planning, wealth management, or whatever you want to call it was not part of my training back in the day, doing business, for me, was never about commissions. People were giving me their hard-earned money and trusting me to invest it wisely—it was as simple as that, and it still is.

It's about doing the right thing for clients and building a reputation around that.

Luckily the industry has changed. The fiduciary approach is a lot more valued today, as people have realized that securities have become commoditized. They want an advisor who doesn't only buy what makes sense, but what complements tax planning, estate planning, and the retirement income side of it—in short, it's got to be comprehensive.

To really do that right, you have to look at everything and plan with the client personally based on their tax bracket, their goals for retirement, and the legacy they want to leave. It's especially important to consider the most tax-advantageous places to take their retirement income from, when they start taking it.

All of that is very different from just selling a specific product or class of product. If you're trained in insurance only, you're going to sell insurance products. Are they best for the client? Or for your own income? I've always believed that if you concern yourself more with the former, the latter takes care of itself.

That's why working as an independent advisor is so important to me. There's no meeting production numbers or sales quotas. It's my business, and I can choose to do a little of something, and nothing of something else. It's really up to me, based on what my analysis indicates is best for each client.

I've devoted my life to knowing what my clients don't know—because contrary to the old saying, when it comes to wealth management, what you don't know *can* hurt you.

As enticing as "taking charge of your finances" or "self-directed investing" may sound, let me assure you: just as the defendant who represents himself is said to have a fool for an attorney, the investor who decides he can manage his wealth better than someone who has done so successfully for hundreds of clients … well, you see where I'm going. And in this chapter, I've hopefully given you a taste of what's gotten me here.

* * *

I'm pretty confident that you'll never guess where the next chapter takes us. Frankly, I surprised myself by choosing to share it, because it's a story I can only describe as amazing.

I'd find it difficult to believe—if it hadn't actually happened to me.

CHAPTER 4

Test Me in This

Bring the whole tithe into the storehouse, that there may
be food in my house. Test me in this, and see if I will not
throw open the floodgates of heaven and pour out so much
blessing that there will not be room enough to store it.

—Malachi 3:10

THE FIRST THREE CHAPTERS have provided insight, I hope, into my background and the philosophy I follow in helping clients plan for personally fulfilling, purpose-driven retirements. But you can't fully comprehend the importance I place on having a higher purpose without understanding what made it a priority in my own life.

It happened as life-changing experiences often do: at the moment it was most needed, and from the last place I expected.

Before I go on, let me be clear: I am not a religious person. I do not regularly attend church. I find God when I pray and when I am reading scripture. And while I believe strongly in the wisdom of the Bible, I never push my beliefs on clients.

If I don't share the following story, however—despite my discomfort with doing so—I'll be ignoring the experience that has given my life purpose and success on a scale I never dreamed possible.

A serious $truggle

It was early 1991. Ken's dental practice was up and running, and I had already left the "wirehouse" firms of Shearson (and later, Prudential Bache) to found D.K. Brede Investment Management Company.

We'd stretched our tiny budget several years before to purchase an even-tinier house to move closer to our work, which meant moving closer to the Boston suburbs. If you know anything about real estate prices in New England, you'll appreciate how, for a young married couple struggling to establish themselves, that was a big deal. Or more accurately, a big *expense*. One we were now doing a bang-up job of making even more costly.

We'd taken out a home equity loan to double the size of the house, taking it from a tiny two-bedroom A-frame—with a kitchen the size of a small hallway—to a three-bedroom house with a place for us to cook a lot more comfortably. We should have done it within budget, but I was doing everything at a higher level.

"I don't just want this standard tile in the bathroom," I'd say. "I'm going to be looking at it the rest of my life. I want something a little bit better." Which, of course, meant more expensive.

Beyond the mortgage, beyond the home equity loan, we'd soon amassed major credit card debt: $75,000, at interest rates ranging from 17 to 26 percent.

If all that wasn't enough, I was pregnant.

We'd been trying for some time. When it was finally confirmed, we were ecstatic. We'd figure out the money, we said. Our businesses would prosper. Everything would be fine. Any couple that has ever been in that situation understands the sort of blind optimism I'm talking about. For us, it was further supported by the fact that we weren't kids anymore.

We'd both worked very hard throughout our twenties and early thirties to get very good at what we did, Ken in dentistry, me in finance. It was only a matter of time before his patient roster blossomed, and before my client base of wealthy clients grew.

It had to be.

"Bad things come in threes"

So I'm maybe four months pregnant, and had just met with a prospective client in downtown Boston.

It hadn't gone well.

Forget morning sickness, I had morning, noon, and nighttime sickness, and this day was no different. I excused myself midpresentation, then came back and finished. But as I walked to my car, all optimism seemed to drain from me. I knew I'd blown it. This prospect was meeting with top brokers from all over Boston and was not likely to go with the bloated gal who couldn't keep her breakfast down. (I am happy to say that the following week, this prospect did hire me as their advisor, and to this day I continue to manage their entire investment portfolio.)

Then I saw the damage.

My new Saab—with a baby on the way, we'd purchased a safe car—was mashed on the passenger's side. There was no note, no nothing. If my mood had been dark before, it was now downright dismal.

As I was driving back to the office, hands on the wheel, I saw it. The stone of my engagement ring. It was gone.

I turned the car around and headed back. I checked the parking lot, the sidewalk, even searched the (cobblestone!) street. No luck, of course. "This day has gone from bad to catastrophic," I thought.

Back at my office, my assistant handed me my messages. "Your doctor's been trying to reach you." My heart sank.

I'd gone in for an amniocentesis test two days before. The doctor said he'd have test results in a couple of weeks, but would call within a couple of days if there was a problem with the preliminary test results. "There's something wrong with the baby," I thought. I tried to call, but he was with a patient.

"Cancel all my appointments," I told my assistant. "I can't take it anymore. I'm going to drive home. If the doctor calls here, tell him to call my house."

I drove my new, damaged car home, glancing occasionally at my stoneless engagement ring and wondering what was wrong with the child we'd tried for so long to conceive. And then, something my mother, who was very superstitious, used to say popped into my head.

"Bad things come in threes."

A bargain

Back at home I sat down, distraught.

"God, if you really exist," I cried out in a prayer, "I ask you to give me a healthy son, and I promise to teach him about you."

I don't know where "son" came from. It wasn't like I preferred a boy over a girl; it just came out. Within seconds of sending up my prayer, the phone rang. It was my doctor.

"Do we have to terminate the pregnancy?" I asked.

"What?" he said. "The baby is fine!"

"Well, why are you calling me? You said it would be two weeks unless something was wrong." I was unconvinced. "Did you do all the tests? I was a biology major in college," I said, and started rattling off everything he should have tested for.

"You were so nervous when you were here for your appointment, I put your test through stat. Everything's fine," he assured me.

Relief washed over me.

"All right then … is it a boy or a girl?"

"Do you really want to know? It'll be a surprise when you have the baby."

"No, believe me, it's as much of a surprise right this minute as it would be when I see the baby," I said. "A boy or girl?"

"It's a boy," he told me.

I thanked him, got off the phone, and went my merry way. I didn't pray, didn't thank God—and before I knew it, my boy was born, and perfect in my eyes. It wasn't until my doctor, making the rounds after delivery, told me everything was good with my baby that it hit me. God had proved himself to be real.

"Oh my God!" I thought. "I've got to teach this baby about God. I know *nothing* about God!"

I only knew what I'd seen in the movies—when people didn't follow his commandments, God would just strike them down. I knew only of an angry God. I was suddenly fearful, thinking, "I've got to figure this out!"

But where to start? Of course. Church!

I began attending services at a nearby church, hoping to find something that had eluded so many before me: the meaning of "God."

The sermons were OK, the congregation friendly. But as the weeks went by, I realized nothing was reaching me. There was no lightbulb moment, nothing I found convincing enough to allow me to teach our child. (We named him Joshua, a name I had always loved. Little did I know at the time that Joshua would lead me to my promised land. Because of him, I searched for and found God.)

After a few more weeks of attending church, it hit me: instead of looking for the meaning of God in the words of others, why not go right to the source?

* * *

I bought a Bible. Actually two; the King James Version confused me with some of the archaic words, expressions, and phrases, so I also purchased a newer translation.

I set my clock to wake up an hour earlier each morning and sat in the quietness of my home library with a hot cup of coffee and my new Bible. Before I started my study, I always made it a point to ask God to teach me and show me the truth. I methodically started at the beginning: the book of Genesis. I worked through every verse, every chapter, each of the Old Testament's thirty-nine books. They were filled with wisdom and moral guidance, much of which I considered, frankly, just the right things to do. Most fascinating to me was learning of the spiritual laws revealed in scripture, which I will talk more of in the final chapter of this book.

One day I got sick with the flu, came home from work, and decided to continue my study of the Bible. I had finally reached the book of Malachi, the last book of the Old Testament, and came upon Malachi 3:10:

Bring the whole tithe into the storehouse, that there may
be food in my house. "Test me in this," the LORD said,
"and see if I will not throw open the floodgates of heaven
and pour out so much blessing that there will not be
room enough to store it."

"Wait," I thought. "What?"

I read it again.

"Test me in this," it read. Through the previous thirty-eight
books, I had never seen that. It was always, "Do *not* test the LORD,
thy God."

Maybe it was a typo. I checked the concordances for both of
my translations of the Bible, under the word "test." After multiple
citations for "Do not test the LORD, thy God," came this one: "Test
me in this." Attributed, just as I'd read in the text itself, to Malachi
3:10.

So I prayed, saying, "I'm going to test you in this, Lord."

This was in 1992, not long after Joshua's birth the year before.
D.K. Brede Investment Management was up and running, and I had
one assistant working for me. Large-cap, blue-growth stocks were
going through a tough time. Everything was still commission-based,
so income was pretty scarce. I'd been leaning heavily on the home
equity line of credit.

Now here I was, at home with this terrible flu and with $1,010
in my business account, which was needed to pay my assistant's
weekly salary. On top of that, my home equity credit line was pretty
much maxed.

What I decided to do after reading this Malachi verse was
actually kind of backward. The idea with tithing is to give 10 percent
of your income as it is received; to bring it "into my house" as the

passage says, meaning the Lord's house. I was determined to test the Lord in tithing. *Right now.*

I think of the Lord's house as not just a church but an organization that does the work of the Lord. Because I read in scripture many times of the importance God put on taking care of the poor and needy, I wrote out a check: $1,000, payable to a well-respected local charity that took care of the homeless. I then addressed the envelope, took it to the mailbox, and walked back to the house, wondering if I'd done the right thing. At the front door, I turned—to see the postman. And it was gone. Done.

Back inside—within minutes *again,* just as when the doctor had called me at home to say everything with my pregnancy was fine—the phone rang. It was my staffer.

"Deb, you're not going to believe this," she said. "You just got hired."

* * *

Months before, while still pregnant with Josh, I'd done a presentation for a state account (regulations prevent me from naming which one). I was competing with the Goldmans, the Vanguards, and eight other firms. Their top people were all giving presentations using PowerPoint when it was still a fairly novel thing.

I didn't have any of that. I came in with several slides, expecting them to have a projector. They didn't.

So I gave my talk without any visual aids—and embraced it. What choice did I have?

"No smoke, no mirrors," I said. "When you're building a state insurance account, you should start by investing in a solid base of bonds, then you have to do this, this, and this." It probably took all of ten minutes. The big guns took half an hour, brought in their investment gurus, and probably put the room to sleep. But at least they had visuals.

I flew back to Boston. "What a waste of time and money," I thought.

But now here was my assistant, telling me differently.

"They want you to call! I told them you're sick, but they said you got it, and they're going to wire in $10 million! They want you to do what you want, in bonds!"

The commission I would make on $10 million worth of bond purchases was $10,000. Ten thousand dollars that I learned I'd be getting within minutes—literally—of putting that $1,000 check to charity in the mail.

Again: "tithe" means "tenth." Talk about paying it forward. Needless to say, I was awestruck.

In the empty room where I was studying, I said, "God, you have shown me that you keep your word." From that day forward, I have tithed my income and trusted God with my financial well-being.

One more hurdle

God's immediate response to my demonstrated charity was all I needed to see. Ken, on the other hand …

"Deb, we don't have the money. There is no way," he said. "We've got so much debt, including this high-interest credit card debt."

I said, "No, it's OK!" He surely thought I'd lost my mind.

"I know we put our money together," I said. "But I'm going to tithe with my income. Do what you want with yours, and we'll put all our money together at the end and see what happens."

Needless to say, my husband was not in favor of my tithing. Then the incredible became the unbelievable.

> **Even though I initially tithed to test God, it soon became evident to me that giving the first tenth of my income felt right. It helped those less fortunate than me and felt good to give back.**

Within one year, we were *totally* out of debt. It was like I was a magnet for new clients, each one wealthier than the last. To this day, I cannot believe the number of clients who were being referred to me, one after the other. Within a year, I no longer had *one* staffer, but two full-time and one part-time. It was amazing. (Today I have nine staffers.)

Nothing else had changed. I did no advertising. I'd even stopped doing seminars to attract new clients, since I had a young baby. And new clients just kept coming.

Since I started giving back, I've always been covered financially—even in bad market conditions. It seems like I not only get through it, but that even more business comes in.

Even though I initially tithed to test God, it soon became evident to me that giving the first tenth of my income felt right. It helped those less fortunate than me and felt good to give back.

* * *

Though I was hesitant to do so, I hope it's now clear why I shared this story. Not only is it still amazing, even to me (and after all these years), but it has worked: tithing passed the test.

What's more, since I began giving back, I've seemed to attract clients who share my belief in leading a purpose-driven life. The intangibles that accrue to those who help make the world a better place are reason enough for doing so, but there are tangible benefits as well: philanthropy is a great tool for wealth preservation, as it is a terrific hedge against taxes.

Yet while I strongly endorse a philanthropic component as part of my clients' overall wealth management strategies, I don't require it. Purpose takes many forms, and I believe it is up to each of us to determine how our wealth can be best applied.

Part two provides tools and information to help you figure that out. We'll start by developing a clear picture of your purpose and goals for retirement. Then, I'll share the strategic approach I have applied in helping hundreds of retirees preserve and expand their wealth and realize their retirement objectives—whatever they might be.

Peace of Mind

CHAPTER 5

What Is Peace of Mind?

I HAVE A CLIENT who *must* have one million dollars, in cash, available at all times. He doesn't really use it; he's got more than he needs to cover his living expenses, thanks to a pension, social security, and more still in real estate income. He'll frankly never need that cash.

Nonetheless, he wants that amount of his investment portfolio kept in cash: maybe to save himself therapy visits. Maybe to help him sleep better at night. Though he isn't spending it, just *knowing* that he has a completely fluid million bucks that does not fluctuate in value has bought him something much more valuable: peace of mind.

In this chapter, we'll take a long look at peace of mind and the crucial role it plays in purpose-driven retirement. No two people define it in exactly the same way (and I've seen a lot of people over the years).

I'll also share some questions I ask clients and use every day in my practice. The answers help me understand what my clients want and need to feel secure in retirement: in other words, what peace of mind means to them. That knowledge is essential in designing an investment strategy that can not only provide them with peace of mind but also help them fund a purpose-driven retirement.

Peace of mind, now and later

Just as the things which put our minds at ease are as unique as each of us, so too do they change at various points in our lives. The biggest turning point I see affecting my clients' fiscal peace of mind is the one this book is all about: retirement.

People bring a totally different mind-set to *saving* for retirement than they do to *living* in retirement.

Often, it's all I can do to drag a client who is still working into my office for an annual review of his portfolio. That's understandable: a doctor who rose early in the morning, made his rounds at the hospital, and then saw ten or twenty patients in his office by late afternoon is bound to be a lot more interested in heading home and resting up—before repeating the routine tomorrow—than in coming to see me at the end of his day.

Once retired, however, that same client may watch his holdings on a daily—or even hourly—basis. He sees his account—*his money!*—rise and fall with the markets, and the fluctuations worry him. "Will my money last? What if it doesn't? Now that I'm retired, I have plenty of time on my hands ... maybe I should take the reins and manage things myself!"

That's nearly always a bad decision, for reasons I'll talk more about in the next chapter. But it does illustrate how actually living in retirement can impact one's peace of mind.

Even my longest-term clients tend to forget that their portfolios have survived through market ups and downs. While they were working, we set up their portfolios for growth, with most of their holdings allocated on the equity side (i.e., invested in the stock market). As they near retirement, we increasingly migrate some of their capital to more stable holdings, like bonds and cash, to help assure they'll have ample funds for the retirement we've planned, even during bad market cycles.

They know all this on one level, of course. Yet the fact that they are no longer producing income, no longer adding to their wealth through work, is enough to negate that knowledge. The result? Worry!

It's not a character flaw. It's human nature; they've flipped a momentous switch, going—literally overnight—from earning money in order to live to living off the money they've earned. It's only natural to wonder if it will last.

That's why, whether you are already retired or still working, the time to be proactive about defining and securing financial peace of mind is *right now*. The two most important steps you can take in doing so are (1) finding and working with an advisor you trust who works to the fiduciary standard, and (2) helping her or him understand what peace of mind means to you so they can direct their work toward helping you lead a rich, vibrant, purpose-driven retirement.

The next two stories[3] show the importance of clearly defining what matters most to you in achieving your retirement goals—*and* of communicating those things to those closest to you.

Richard and Mary

My client Richard retired from a Fortune 500 company with a really generous pension. He and his wife, Mary, had also accumulated around two million dollars in 401(k) savings and in other, nonretirement savings.

---

3   The client stories included are for illustrative purposes only. Actual performance and results will vary. Names and details have been changed for the protection of clients. These examples do not constitute a recommendation as to the suitability of any investment for any person or persons having circumstances similar to those portrayed. A financial advisor should be consulted regarding your specific circumstances.

Richard had a company pension which, together with the couple's combined social security benefit, covered their current and projected living expenses. The funds to travel and to fulfill their other bucket-list goals for retirement, however, had to come from income and growth on their savings.

They also had differing objectives of *purpose* which, left unresolved, could have become a real bone of contention between them. Mary wanted a vacation house on Cape Cod, where their kids and grandkids could come for vacation and build lasting family memories. Richard was all about education. His top priority was helping their grandkids pay their college expenses.

The solution to these seemingly divergent goals came when we all sat down in my office. It took a lot of back and forth; a lot of each seeing the other's point of view. That had been difficult for Richard and Mary alone. But with an objective third party guiding the discussion—one who had helped hundreds of people think in new ways about achieving their retirement goals—they were able to see opportunities which, absent that third-party perspective, had eluded them.

I told them that if they could find a vacation home for around $750,000, it would leave enough in savings to provide the income and growth they would need to cover the cost of both carrying this house and of the travel they wanted to do in their retirement. I also recommended that they save into 529 plans any extra money they did not spend each year. Since their eldest grandchild would not start college for another nine years, when that time came, they would sell the vacation house and use the proceeds to cover the upcoming college tuition payments—making it possible for their grandkids to start their careers with no college loans to pay off.

Mary found the Cape Cod vacation home she dreamed of building family memories in. I am happy to say that because of their disciplined planning and their saving regularly the excess they did not spend each year, they will more than likely be able to keep this vacation home for many, many more years.

Mark and Jan

Another client couple of mine who were financially well off, with enough income from their savings and investments to cover the costs of maintaining both a Boston condo and their home on the coast of Maine, came to me with different financial concerns.

Mark and Jan had four children, all of whom had long since left the nest. As one of the nation's leading orthopedic surgeons, Mark understood the value of a great education and had worked hard to give one to each of the couple's children. They had attended the best private schools and universities; two had degrees from Ivy League institutions. All were leading successful careers.

Their children gave the couple seven terrific grandkids, and Mark and Jan were living the retirement I'd helped them prepare for. They made memories with their kids and grandkids in Maine. The eldest grandchild, now a young man, had recently enrolled in a top private university.

But one morning, I got a frantic call from Jan. She and Mark needed to see me right away, she said, the distress in her voice all too obvious.

"Of course!" I said, wondering what was up. "I can squeeze you in this afternoon."

We'd no sooner sat down than Jan laid an invoice on my desk: a tuition bill for her grandson's college studies. Apparently, his father—Mark and Jan's son—had assumed his parents would be paying for this grandchild's education. And he wasn't alone.

Mark's success as a surgeon had apparently convinced all his kids that he had massive stores of wealth. After all, he'd not only put each of them through the best schools and colleges but raised them in one of Boston's toniest neighborhoods. Maybe that upbringing had shielded them from knowing the true cost of such things. (Of course, it's not hard to find out—nor to multiply that cost seven times. But I digress.)

Mark and Jan needed to protect their own financial security, and I told them so. "It's time for a family meeting," I said.

I've never studied family dynamics or counseling, but circumstances like this one have helped me get pretty good at both—especially when years of work toward securing a client's retirement and legacy are about to be wiped away.

So, in they came: the couple's four kids, their spouses, and Mark and Jan themselves. We sat them down and commenced educating them about the cost of an education—and what it would mean if Mark were to pay the college expenses of seven grandkids.

To their credit, the couple's children immediately understood.

"We just can't expect them to do this," the daughter told the group. The son whose child was about to start college spoke up and owned the role he might have played, as the eldest, in signaling to his siblings that Dad could afford to do it.

"I was wrong," he said. "It would mean Mom and Dad would have to give up either the Maine house or the condo in Boston."

In the end, Mark and Jan said they would help as they could, perhaps giving $5,000 a year to each grandkid while they were in college. But they didn't want an ironclad agreement. They made it clear that they'd devoted their working lives to providing their children with the tools to succeed. Now it was up to them to do the same for their kids.

"At our stage of life," Mark told his family, "we must first protect our own financial security. Each of you has your whole life to do the same: to prepare your children and feather your own nests for retirement." Then, with a chuckle, he added: "Just be sure *your* kids understand much sooner what you have learned today!"

A million dollars sounds like a lot of money, but putting seven grandchildren through top universities will burn through twice that amount—and that's assuming tuition stops rising right now (as if!). When Mark and Jan realized the impact of losing that money on their retirement plans—in terms of the capital itself and the investment income it could produce—they knew that protecting it was their only option.

* * *

These two stories share some common elements: a retired couple with grown children, grandchildren, and some hard decisions to make. Despite their very different, situationally appropriate resolutions, both outcomes hinged on the same thing: honest communication.

Richard and Mary did not realize their imperatives for retirement were so different. But once they were on the table, we found a way to satisfy them both, building family memories and putting their grandkids through college.

Mark and Jan had a shared vision: giving their kids the best possible upbringing, on the expectation that they would do the same for their own children. Though they were stunned when that tuition bill arrived, it was immediately clear where the breakdown had occurred: they'd been so focused on leading by example that they'd neglected to *spell out* their grown kids' responsibilities.

I won't pretend that all couples are as accommodating of each other as Richard and Mary, or that all kids are as understanding as

Mark and Jan's. But I *can* assure you that pinning down all your expectations for retirement by clearly defining what peace of mind looks like for you—and *communicating* that to those you care about, in no uncertain terms—is critical to protecting the wealth you've established and making purpose-driven retirement a reality.

Now that you understand the task before you, let's take some steps toward accomplishing it!

What does peace of mind mean to you?

Each portfolio I create is like a tailored suit: customized to the client's needs. To do that right, we begin with a frank conversation about the client's goals for both their retirement years and their estate—the legacy they'll leave behind.

We discuss their hopes, dreams, and fears. Their level of comfort with risk. Their families' expectations, real and assumed. And not least, what *each client* wants to achieve when his or her working days are done: their *purpose* in retirement. This question is often overlooked, yet without purpose, any retirement can quickly morph into something just this side of torture, for reasons I'll explain a little later.

My initial conversation with a new client gives me a clear picture of what peace of mind means to them. Without it, I can't meet the fiduciary responsibility with which they'll entrust me. So we cover everything in detail and then review it, to be certain we're of one mind.

Then, I go a step further.

I explain various approaches to managing the client's wealth *relative* to the goals we've established. Then, I watch their reactions—like a hawk. This crystallizes their comfort level and tells me how far I can go in pursuit of their objectives; where the line exists between

"Richard and Mary are fine with this level of risk in equities, let's buy" and "I'd better have more meetings and take this allocation into equities more slowly."

Defining peace of mind

Understanding what peace of mind means for the client is my primary goal for the first meeting. I pursue it not with a generic risk profile questionnaire used by the financial services industry, but through a set of metrics I've mentally cultivated and maintained over thirty-three years of meeting literally thousands of potential clients.

You see, risk is not something investors can afford to get wrong. If they take too little risk, they can limit the growth of their investment portfolio.

I have found that risk tolerance questionnaires are not equipped to account for how emotions drive decision-making. And a misunderstanding of some of the questions can cause the one being questioned to answer inappropriately, leading to an incorrect risk profile.

You see, risk is not something investors can afford to get wrong. If they take too little risk, they can limit the growth of their investment portfolio. If they take too much, they may not be able to handle the volatility of the portfolio, and sell out when the markets drop. I find that getting it right requires an in-depth discussion.

The metrics I use cover everything I absolutely must know in order to do the best possible job for the client, whatever their circumstances might be. Because while clients' primary concerns are often similar, their situations are seldom the same.

As you read through the questions which follow and my reasons for asking them, I hope you'll also ask them of yourself. Later, I'll offer you a chance to receive a complimentary, confidential peace of mind assessment through my website, Debrabrede.com.

Topping my must-know list: **"What is your biggest fear when it comes to retirement?"**

This goes straight to peace of mind. Typical fears are running out of money, health issues, and the cost of travel to keep up with family, whether the client moves away for retirement or their kids do, for career or lifestyle reasons.

Next: **"What amount of retirement savings do you need to feel financially secure?"**

This is where things get interesting. One answer I get all the time: "Ten million bucks." (For some reason, it's an especially popular number with doctors.)

"OK," I say. "Why?"

Of course, they have no idea.

When we drill down and look at lifestyle, purpose, family obligations, the whole nine yards, maybe he only needs four million. Or two. Or six. Whatever it may be. But here's the thing: we actually *figure it out.*

I had a surgeon come in. He had three homes and couldn't save a nickel outside of his 401(k) due to his high discretionary spending. But his 401(k) had just hit $1 million—and he said, "OK, I'm ready to retire."

I said, "No you're not. You need several more million." I reminded him of the 4 percent rule. It states that a 4 percent annual distribution rate is what most consultants to Wall Street firms figured was a safe amount, based on a portfolio with 50 percent in equities, 40 percent in bonds, and 10 percent in cash. The consensus is that someone retired for thirty years would not run out of money in their lifetime. See sustainable withdrawal rate chart.

Excess Withdrawal

Sustainable withdrawal rates can extend the life of a portfolio

How a couple retiring in 1972 with $500,000 is affected.

50% STOCK, 40% BONDS, 10% SHORT-TERM INVESTMENTS 1972–2012

Withdrawals are inflation adjusted*

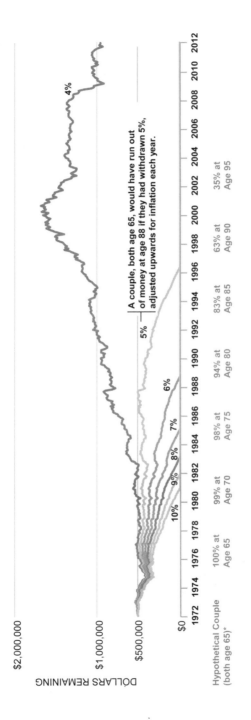

A couple, both age 65, would have run out of money at age 88 if they had withdrawn 5%, adjusted upwards for inflation each year.

| Hypothetical Couple (both age 65)* | 100% at Age 65 | 99% at Age 70 | 98% at Age 75 | 94% at Age 80 | 83% at Age 85 | 63% at Age 90 | 35% at Age 95 |

Source: Fidelity Investments. Hypothetical value of assets held in an untaxed account of $500,000 invested in a portfolio of 50% stocks, 40% bonds, and 10% short-term investments with inflation-adjusted withdrawal rates as specified. This chart uses historical monthly performance from January 1972 through December 2012 from Ibbotson Associates; stocks, bonds, and short-term investments are represented by the S&P 500, U.S. Intermediate-Term Government Bonds, and U.S. 30-day T-bills, respectively. You cannot invest directly in an index. This chart is for illustrative purposes only, is not indicative of any investment, and is not intended to project or predict the present or future value of the actual holdings in a participant's portfolio or the performance of a given model portfolio of securities. Past performance is no guarantee of future results.

* Probability of a couple surviving to various ages is based on Annuity 2000 Mortality Table, Society of Actuaries. Figures assume a person is in good health.

Please see disclosure for the
Excess Withdrawal chart on page 74.

Important: The projections regarding the likelihood of various investment outcomes are hypothetical in nature, do not reflect actual investment results, and are not guarantees of future results. Results may vary with each use and over time. Although past performance does not guarantee future results, it may be useful in comparing alternative investment strategies over the long term. Performance returns for actual investments will generally be reduced by fees or expenses not reflected in these hypothetical illustrations.

The chart on page 73 is not intended to project or predict the present or future value of the actual holdings in a participant's portfolio or the performance of a given model portfolio of securities.

Methodology and information: For the chart shown on page 73, which highlights varying levels of stocks, bonds, and short-term investments, the purpose of this hypothetical illustration is to show how portfolios may be created with different risk and return characteristics to help meet a participant's goals. You should choose your own investments based on your particular objectives and situation. Remember, you may change how your account is invested. Be sure to review your decisions periodically to make sure they are still consistent with your goals. You should also consider all of your investments when making your investment choices.

All index returns include reinvestment of dividends and interest income. It is not possible to invest directly in any of the indices described above. Investors may be charged fees when investing in an actual portfolio of securities, which are not reflected in illustrations utilizing returns of market indices.

Index Definitions: Standard & Poor's 500 Index (S&P 500) is a market capitalization-weighted index of 500 widely held U.S. stocks and includes reinvestment of dividends.

U.S. Intermediate-Term Government Bond Index is an unmanaged index that includes the reinvestment of interest income. U.S Treasury bills are backed by the full faith and credit of the U.S government.

With a million in a retirement plan, this surgeon and his wife would have to live on forty grand a year, plus social security. This was barely enough to cover the expenses on *one* of those houses, in addition to their other necessary living expenses such as food, autos, supplemental medical coverage, etcetera. Also, he would not have the funds needed to allow him to do all the stuff he liked to do. He was making $500,000 a year, but had no savings outside that 401(k).

There's one reason I ask the "how much do you need" question: to see if the client has given any reality-based thought whatsoever to their needs. If that sounds harsh, so be it, because in my experience, the vast majority of people have not, and throw out a number that is totally arbitrary. And it goes in both directions: I'm telling people "you don't need that much" just as often as I'm saying "you need more." Either way, it's much easier to get their attention by beginning with what *they think* they need.

Of course, there's a third possibility: they don't need a plan at all. It's rare, but it does happen. Some people have such wealth that planning would be silly. I look at their lifestyles, at what they're spending, and it's obvious: they'll be fine. They don't need some hundred-page plan to convince them, "Oh my God! *Whew!* It's in writing, so I can feel good about it."

Next, I refine things further: **"What amount of *income* do you need to live *comfortably*?"**

They might answer, $200,000. But that's their *current income,* while they're still working—and paying FICA taxes and contributing to a 401(k). I want to know how much they expect to need *in retirement.* If the house is paid off. Or not. If they plan to live here, where property taxes can kill you, or there, where they're next to nothing.

Without answers to such questions, I can't devise a plan.

Of course, there are firms out there that will anyway. They bring people in and put together plans, some even robotically. The person fills out a long form with generic questions, and the firm spits out a "financial plan" they've charged a couple grand for (or that the firm sometimes does it for free). Then, the firm's financial advisor puts the client in one of six portfolios made up of predetermined equities and bonds, invested via either mutual funds or separate holdings.

All the portfolios contain the same equities and same bonds, with the equity allocation set at 100, 80, 60, 40, 20, or 0 percent and the remainder in bonds. Then the firm sells the client some insurance or annuities, and they're done. It's like going to an automated car wash; you're just deciding if you want the hot wax or Rain-X.

That's not planning, and it certainly isn't wealth management. Unless, of course, we're talking about the *firm's* wealth.

Something else I want clients to tell me: **"What do you look forward to doing in retirement?"**

It makes a difference. For an avid golfer, or a foodie, retirement is going to be a lot more expensive than it will be for a person who is happy to visit the local library and plow through a stack of books in a backyard hammock, frosty drink in hand.

Then: **"What does *financial independence* mean to you?"**

Forty or fifty years of work leaves many people so accustomed to getting a regular check that the prospect of *not* getting one scares them to death, so it's what they want to see in retirement. Others, like the client I described at the start of the chapter, want to have a million bucks sitting in their money market account at all times. Financial independence means different things to different people, and a big part of my job is helping people achieve their definition of it.

I also want to know: **"What will you miss about your job?"**

One of my clients was a high-powered attorney who worked seventy hours a week—and that's when he was almost seventy years old! He simply loved his job; it was his life. His wife finally talked him into retiring, which in itself was a real process: it meant extricating himself from his current cases and getting others in the firm up to speed on them.

When he finally retired, it was terribly rough. His job was why he'd gotten up each morning; it got his juices flowing, like someone who plays tennis every day, and suddenly that was gone. He did not play golf and had no real hobbies or interests outside of his profession. His work was his life.

His wife had her girlfriends, with their regular lunch dates and other activities. Even though she had wanted him to retire, she had not planned on spending all her time with him. He'd call me and ask, "Deb, what newspapers do you read?" And I gave him three names, but then told him that after reading the first two, the third is just more of the same. He'd then call at a different time and ask, "What good books have you read? What are you up to?" He was bored. Retirement proved too passive for him.

Then he realized that retirement offered a way to keep doing what he loved but to the benefit of people in need. He started taking cases pro bono and stopped driving his wife (and his financial advisor) crazy as he searched in vain for something to hold his attention.

Asking potential clients what they'll miss about their work helps them see retirement not as the end of something but the beginning of something new and purposeful—often with the talents and passions that made them successful in their careers.

There's also my bucket-list question: **"If you knew you would die tomorrow, what would you regret not doing?"**

Would you wish you had seen the Grand Canyon? Gone to Paris and spent time at the Louvre? Whatever it might be.

Here's one that always gets an interesting response: **"If money was no object, what would you do?"**

I like this one because it offers insight into the client's aspirations while at the same time grounding them. They might say, "I'd buy my kids apartments in New York." They might also say, "I want to get back into a size two bathing suit." (I know I would, but at age sixty-two, it ain't gonna happen!)

I also delve into purpose: **"What would you like to experience or accomplish in retirement?"**

This one often produces inspiring answers, from starting a nonprofit to traveling to new places. One of my clients is going to chef school; he is just so into cooking that he wanted to be trained classically in French cuisine. His wife loves it, too, except for the effects of all that butter (speaking of swimsuit sizes). But seriously, it's a good thing for both of them. It keeps them going.

I find many of my clients enjoy taking classes at their local colleges. They not only learn new and interesting things, but end up meeting a lot of new people that become friends.

Often when I ask this question, however, I get a more typical response: "Absolutely nothing. I plan to bring new meaning to the words *leisure activities.*"

I'll admit, the idea of fishing, playing golf, sailing, or engaging in *any* leisure activity—all day, every day—looks incredibly appealing to most people. *While they are still working.* But two or three or six months into such a routine, it becomes ... well, routine. And it's a very short step from there to boredom.

Maybe you're saying, "Well, that's true for *most* people. But I'm different! I do all those things, and more! I'll just alternate among them for variety. Boredom? I don't think so!"

OK. But have you considered the *cost*? The boat, the country club dues, the excursions to exotic fishing holes? It's actually easier to afford leisure activities while you're still adding to your wealth—through employment—than when you're drawing from it in retirement. Disabusing clients of the opposite notion consumes much of my time.

Here's a biggie: **"Do you want to leave an inheritance?"**

People cover the whole map on this one, too. "I put my kids through the best colleges, I've given them everything," some say. "The rest is up to them." Even Warren Buffett has said he's not leaving his kids all his millions. Though I'm confident they'll never be uncomfortable, he is strongly insistent that they do something with their lives.

Then again, leaving an inheritance doesn't have to mean being irresponsible, or encouraging its recipient to be. Lots of people do it prudently, which, in terms of their own retirements, is the key—because *they* still have lives to live.

Some retirees can live happily on a 4 percent distribution from their portfolio each year. I have a retired client who is fifty years old and takes 5 percent a year. She could live to 100 and be just fine. But if her goal were to leave each of her kids half a million bucks, we'd be doing things very differently. (See the box "Inheritance Planning" for a detailed discussion of this.)

INHERITANCE PLANNING

I place a priority on discussing with clients how best to leave an inheritance to their loved ones so we can plan accordingly.

For instance, Roth accounts are advantageous to inherit, in that the assets continue to grow untaxed and withdrawals are tax free. Even though the beneficiary of the inherited Roth must begin taking required minimum distributions (RMDs) annually by December thirty-first of the year after the year in which the owner died, the corpus of the Roth continues to grow, tax free.

If the children (or other beneficiary) you designated are in a higher tax bracket than you, it's smart to consider doing a Roth conversion with part of your retirement assets.

You see, if your beneficiaries are still working at the time of your death, even if they are under fifty-nine and a half years old, they must still take annual RMDs from an inherited, non-Roth retirement account. Those RMDs would be counted as current income, potentially throwing them into the highest federal tax bracket and adding to their tax burden at the state level too. In short, they're just going to get killed with taxes.

I often look at the retiree's current tax bracket and calculate with their accountant the amount we can safely convert into a Roth without putting the retiree into a higher bracket. Sometimes, it is only $10,000 or $20,000 of IRA assets that we are able to convert into a Roth, but even that amount will help your beneficiary.

With the 2018 tax law change, I helped married clients convert as much as $150,000 and stay in the same tax bracket they were in the year before, meaning that $150,000 moved out of their IRAs and reduced the future RMD amounts from those IRAs. Plus, while they are alive, they incur no RMD responsibility on their Roth. Even better, this $150,000 can now grow in the Roth without future tax—to them or their beneficiaries. This is a win, win, win situation.

If your retirement account beneficiary is in a lower tax bracket than you, however, this strategy is more than likely unnecessary.

For the retiree in a high tax bracket, it usually makes no sense to do a Roth conversion. But it does make sense to use the retiree's RMD to fund part or all of their charitable contributions. (Note that the RMD check must be made payable to the charity.) This not only allows the retiree to avoid paying income taxes on the RMD amount but preserves their nonretirement funds. I have found that most people use their nonretirement assets, such as their checking accounts, to write checks to the charities they support.

Nonretirement assets are next in line, after Roth accounts, as another desirable asset to leave your loved ones. Upon the death of the owner, the assets in a nonretirement account receive a stepped-up "basis"—in other words, the value of the assets on the owner's date of death become the new cost basis, for tax purposes, for the beneficiary. That means they inherit the market appreciation the account experienced during the decedent's life without paying tax on it.

I have seen many cases in my career of an elderly parent holding shares of a blue-chip stock with a very low cost basis. This is because we bought the stock for them many years ago, and the stock's price has increased over that time. I caution that elderly parent NOT to gift any of the stock while they are living to their children or grandchildren, as those receiving the gift will pick up their cost basis.

For example, if the elderly parent bought Johnson & Johnson stock thirty years ago, they would have paid around five dollars per share (using a split adjusted price). If this elderly parent gifted any of these shares, the person receiving the gift would now own a stock trading, thirty years later, at around one hundred forty-five dollars per share (J&J's price at the time of the writing). If the gift recipient sold the stock right after receiving the gift, they would have to pay capital gains taxes on the one hundred forty-dollar gain per share. For clients with estate tax issues who want to gift some of their appreciated stock to a grandchild, I often recommend that they instead sell the stock in their own name, pay the capital gains tax (this will reduce their own estate taxes), and use the proceeds to gift cash to their grandchild or use the cash to buy new J&J stock for the child. It may sound like a lot of work, but this way, the grandchild is getting the full value of the gift, not something that will see a big bite taken out in taxes when they sell.

The final but most important thing I need to know from clients is this:

"What, as your financial advisor, can I do to give you peace of mind?"

Some will say, "Deb, I just need you to call me once a year and tell me I'm OK, and on track." In fact, I have one client who takes that to the extreme: "If you think I'm spending too much and am at risk of running out of money," he says, "I want you to call me, AND to follow up with a letter, in big red type, saying 'DO NOT SPEND ONE DIME OVER THIS AMOUNT!'"

What can I say? Some people are good at managing their money. Others—not so much. And still others ... oy.

I've had several clients over the years with whom I've spent a lot of time and energy not only educating on the markets' cycles but building what I believed to be beautifully balanced portfolios that would meet their retirement goals and distribution needs. Sadly, these same clients have decimated their portfolios' returns by calling my office and demanding their investment holdings be sold out of the market, simply because financial news channels are having a heyday on the latest downturn in the stock market.

I will discuss this in greater detail in the next chapter, but I can't stress it enough: advertisers are going to pay for ads where audiences tune in.

I personally only watch The Weather Channel when I am about to travel and have heard that a big storm may be brewing. Yet local news channels take that same storm forecast and ramp it up many notches, to the point where the local grocery stores are sold out of bread, milk, and chicken (I know, because I am usually the last to get to the grocery store as I drive home from work with light snow already on the ground).

Now, weather forecasting has come a long way in recent years (although I still hate the way that potentially catastrophic storms are milked by the weather industry for advertising revenue). But financial forecasts—especially those which just gin up investor anxiety for no good reason—are a *genuine threat* to people's retirements; I believe a far greater one than the (supposed) volatility of the markets themselves.

As you'll see in the next chapter, it is ridiculous—to anyone with any grasp of the cyclical nature of markets—to think they can time their purchases and sales of investments with enough consistency to make appreciable gains. Not only do you need to get out before the market drops, you need to get back in before the rebound starts. No one in the history of Wall Street has been able to do this consistently. Usually some take credit for getting you out in time, but those same market gurus miss out on getting you back in in time to take advantage of the market rebound! In other words, you would have been better off not listening and staying the course. This is why I preach "balance, balance, balance" to all my retirees. If you keep enough in bonds and cash to get through the down market turns, you will be fine.

Peace of mind is different for everyone

For one client, peace of mind means having enough income to stay in their house until they die. For another, it's being able to fly two thousand miles to see their grandkids—every month. And for another, it may mean having enough retirement savings that they will not ever need to worry about running out of money in their lifetime, or covering their medical bills and home health care expenses in their later years.

> My job is structuring investment strategies that help give my clients peace of mind, however they define it.

My job is structuring investment strategies that help give my clients peace of mind, however they define it. But retirement means more than peace of mind—more, in fact, than financial security. One question matters more than all those I've shared in this chapter, and it is this:

What's your Act Two?

I work with many retirees in their forties and fifties, people who achieved great success at a young age and are living the dream of early retirement.

But even these folks, for whom the cost of leisure will never be an issue, find—anywhere from six months to a couple of years later—that they've fished themselves into terminal boredom. Or discover that, to have any shot at all of *actually* playing on the senior PGA Tour, they'll have to hit *another* million golf balls. (*And* hope that their back holds up!)

So, as this book's title asks: *Now what?*

If you'd like to begin the work of really answering that question, I invite you to visit **Debrabrede.com**. There you'll find a complimentary, fully confidential listing of the questions raised in this chapter, with a host of answers to each. At minimum, the exercise will get you thinking about matters you probably should have been thinking about already. And if you opt to complete the survey, I'll provide a confidential assessment—including the range of monthly income you're likely to need in retirement in order to live the retirement your answers indicate.

If you'd prefer for now to continue reading, terrific! But begin at least to mull over the questions I've raised. Answering them is the critical first task in securing peace of mind, whatever it looks like for you. With that in place, you'll see that *doing more* is possible. Which is good, because for highly successful, purpose-driven people, living a life of ease in retirement is usually a lot less fun than it sounds.

Like any retirement, a purpose-driven one comes at a price. Meeting it requires faith in your advisor—and a basic understanding of the way markets function, so fears over their day-to-day volatility don't derail your plans.

In chapter 6, I'll get you up to speed.

The Power of Dispassion

Trusting the Markets' Cycles

NOT TOO LONG AGO, I got a call from a reporter at what is widely considered one of the country's leading financial journals. He wanted to talk about Will Danoff.

Now, I have tremendous respect for Will. Not only has he managed Fidelity's Contrafund to become one of the largest actively managed stock mutual funds guided by a single manager (with, at this writing, over $130 billion in assets under management), but he's run it for nearly a quarter of a century (talk about a track record!).

Let me stop and make one thing clear: I am not recommending you buy any mutual fund or investment I write about in this book. It is imperative to read the prospectus before making any investment and to talk with a financial advisor. OK? OK. And now that the compliance folks are happy, my story continues ...

Will has been called a contrarian. What, you might wonder, does that mean?

Remember Danny, my stock market mentor, who I told you about in chapter 3? How, when the Chernobyl nuclear plant blew in

1986 and other brokers were selling their clients out of electric utility stocks, I—a newly minted broker—looked over at Danny and said, "Buying opportunity"?

That's what being a contrarian means.

Rather than hug an index (i.e., buy similar holdings in an index yet in slightly different percentages, as some active managers do), Danoff looks for opportunities which others are ignoring: specific stocks that may be significantly undervalued, whether in the currently trending sector or whole different industries. Companies whose fundamentals are sound and whose products are poised for greater demand. In other words: bargains.

And Danoff has been managing with this mind-set, singlehandedly, for Fidelity's flagship fund for nearly thirty years. He is a widely recognized mutual fund manager.

But this reporter seemed skeptical. Something about his approach—combined, I'm sure, with watching the impact of the financial media grow throughout my career—suggested to me that his paper was looking for a contrarian piece on Danoff, the contrarian.

"What do you think about him?" the reporter finally asked.

"I liked how, back in in the late 1990s, Danoff sold off a good amount of technology stocks," I began. "He thought the sector was overpriced. Then, when the tech-bubble burst in the spring of 2000, Danoff was a hero. Look," I said, "past performance is certainly no guarantee. But he saw what other growth managers did not see, and it paid off!"

The reporter pressed on.

"Well more recently, I'm seeing what looks like a negative trend in his performance."

"Based on what?" I asked.

He says, "I'm looking at one- and three-year returns, and he's underperforming the broader indices."

"Wait," I said, "One year and three years? That's not even one market cycle. How can you judge something against the broader market without using a *full market cycle* as the yardstick?"

In the silence that followed, I could almost hear the lightbulb blink on above the reporter's head. (Did I mention—we were *on the phone!*) And finally he says, "Hmmm. Good point."

Purveyors of passion

That story illustrates the near-total lack of attention paid to market cycles in assessing investment performance, even among those who are *paid to know and report on* investment performance.

That's because the more passionate their presentation, the more likely people will be to listen, watch, or read—and ears and eyeballs are the currency of the realm in today's specialized media landscape. So outlets, with time to fill 24/7/365—including the financial media—have largely followed the model pioneered in the prior century by the general news media: if it bleeds (or looks like it *might* be bleeding), it leads.

Think about it. Are you more likely to buy a newspaper headlined "Everything's fine" or one screaming "The end is near!"

But when it comes to financial reporting, there's a problem: ninety-nine times out of one hundred, everything *is* fine. And on those rare occasions that things get wacky, they are seldom as bad as the media's passionate coverage suggests. Nonetheless, when individual investors choose to pay attention, they can *really* wind up paying.

It's bad enough when someone who has not yet retired scrambles to get out of a plummeting security. He's not only ignoring Wall Street's oldest axiom—buy low, sell high—but he's also ignoring the fact that issues which go down—provided they are fundamentally strong—come back up.

But at least *that* investor can recapitalize his portfolio with future paychecks.

> It is often the combination of too much time and money on one's hands that quickly leads to less of both.

Not so the guy whose working days are over. If *he* allows passion to rule his investment decisions, he's risking capital that's much more difficult to replace.

There are plenty of passionate points of view just waiting to assault retirees who go looking for them. Simply tune to one of the cable networks that cover the markets day and night. Or—if you really feel like climbing out on a ledge—visit several. If you're retired, you certainly have the time.

And therein lies the problem: it is often the combination of too much time and money on one's hands that quickly leads to less of both. Before he knows it, a retiree can find himself hanging on some talking head's every word about Asian markets—at two in the morning—convinced his assets are about to become worthless.

In fact, the markets' daily swings have little, and usually no, bearing on long-term investment success. No matter how passionate or animated your favorite analyst might become.

Understanding what really drives investment performance requires a *dispassionate* approach, and gaining familiarity with market cycles is a great place to start. (Another is judicious use of that button on your TV's remote. The one that says "power.")

What market cycles are, and why they matter

For anyone who worked in the markets or had money in them at the time, the global financial crisis of 2008 was a roller coaster ride. The same goes for the tech-bubble burst of 2000 and the Black Monday crash of 1987.

Each of these events is etched in my memory. Not for their long-term effects, which proved negligible (except for those that jumped out of the market in fear or owned stocks in companies that were not fundamentally sound), but for the mass hysteria they produced.

In 2008, for example, I took panicked calls from clients who'd owned stocks for decades and nearly bought into the panic myself. I'd ask God for wisdom constantly. I knew holding on and buying more was the right course. After all, what a buying opportunity! But when everyone around you is going crazy, doubts of your own sanity come with the turf. Articulating to clients that even this—the global financial crisis—would pass was no mean feat. What could I say to help them feel comfortable?

I needed—and they needed me—to be the voice of reason. So I studied companies that I thought should be benefiting, in a market where people felt poor as they watched their investments' net worth drop with each downward tick of the stock market.

One stock I studied was Costco. I noticed that even my richest clients were suddenly shopping there. One, who lived in a penthouse, excitedly told me about her first-ever trip to Costco with her equally as wealthy girlfriend. All I could picture was the huge bottle of ketchup taking up room in her refrigerator until it expired and the twenty-five rolls of paper towels jammed in her beautiful penthouse's kitchen cabinets. But she felt great about the savings!

Given the level of panic people were experiencing, it was understandable, and sure enough, shares of Costco and even McDonald's were getting hit, *in spite of more people purchasing their products.* In fact, the drop in their stock prices was not in line with their earnings. People were looking for bargains out in the real world, and I was finding them on Wall Street in the same places they were.

But were they worth the effort? My clients were already in (painstakingly) balanced portfolios, partly to help protect them from events like this. I kept faith that the storm would pass. This chart shows why:

Ibbotson® SBBI®
Stocks, Bonds, Bills, and Inflation 1926–2018

Source: Small Stocks—represented by the Ibbotson® Small Company Stock Index; Large Stocks—Ibbotson® Large Company Stock Index; Long-Term Government Bonds—20-year U.S. Government Bond; Treasury Bills—30-day U.S. Treasury Bill; Inflation—Consumer Price Index.

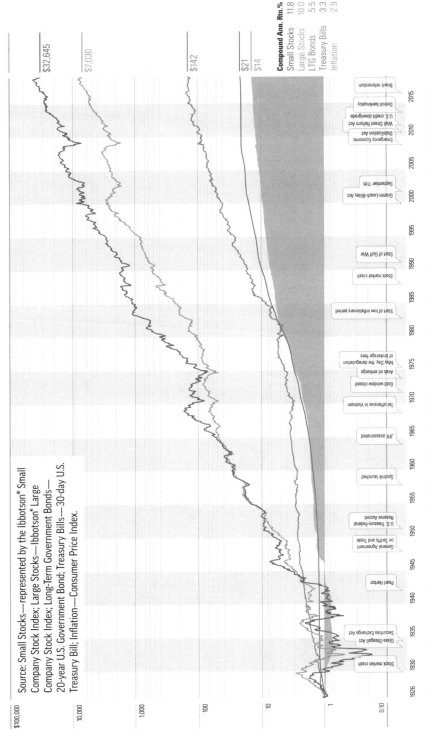

	Compound Ann. Rtn.%
Small Stocks	11.8
Large Stocks	10.0
LTG Bonds	5.5
Treasury Bills	3.3
Inflation	2.9

$32,645

$7,030

$142

$21

$14

Past performance is no guarantee of future results. Hypothetical value of $1 invested at the beginning of 1926. Assumes reinvestment of income and no transaction costs or taxes. This data is for illustrative purposes only and not indicative of any investment. An investment cannot be made directly in an index.

MORNINGSTAR®

93

The vertical graph lines break out market performance in five-year increments. As you can see, stocks and bonds have finished consistently—and markedly—higher at the end of most periods.

Market cycles make the distinction even more stark. What are they, exactly?

A market cycle is period measured not by dates but by market conditions. A cycle is considered complete, or "full," when the market in question has gone from bull to bear and back again to bull.

Although past performance is no guarantee of future results, I believe studying the history of the stock markets' uptrends and declines can help one to better understand why staying invested for the long term can be beneficial.

Using the historical performance of the S&P 500 Index from 1926 through June 2018, the average bull market period lasted 9.1 years, with an average cumulative return of 476 percent. During this same period, the average bear market lasted 1.4 years, with an average cumulative loss of 41 percent.[4]

Yet with all these expansions and contractions, here we still are, with a stock market valuation higher than where it started in 1926. Which brings me to why market cycles matter.

When that reporter called me about Will Danoff and I called him out for not looking at a full market cycle, he had nowhere to go. He was dealing with someone who understands that *the first rule of judging investment performance accurately* is comparing apples to apples—and I'd quickly recognized the orange he'd thrown on the table.

---

4   Source: First Trust Advisors L.P., Morningstar. Returns from 1926–6/29/18. The S&P 500 Index is an unmanaged index of 500 stocks used to measure large-cap US stock market performance. Investors cannot invest directly in an index. Index returns do not reflect any fees, expenses, or sales charges. These returns were the result of certain market factors and events which may not be repeated in the future. Past performance is no guarantee of future results.

The reliability of market cycles—and the power of a contrarian approach—become even clearer when one looks at indexed market returns during difficult periods.

INVESTING DURING UNCERTAIN TIMES

HISTORICAL MOVEMENT OF THE S&P 500 INDEX (1939–2018)

Annual Total Returns (%)															
1939	-0.4	1949	18.6	1959	12.0	1969	-8.4	1979	18.4	1989	31.7	1999	21.0	2009	26.5
1940	-9.8	1950	31.5	1960	0.5	1970	3.9	1980	32.4	1990	-3.1	2000	-9.1	2010	15.1
1941	-11.6	1951	24.0	1961	26.9	1971	14.2	1981	-4.9	1991	30.5	2001	-11.9	2011	2.1
1942	20.1	1952	18.2	1962	-8.7	1972	19.0	1982	21.5	1992	7.6	2002	-22.1	2012	16.0
1943	25.6	1953	-0.9	1963	22.8	1973	-14.7	1983	22.5	1993	10.1	2003	28.7	2013	32.4
1944	19.5	1954	52.3	1964	16.4	1974	-26.3	1984	6.2	1994	1.3	2004	10.9	2014	13.7
1945	36.3	1955	31.4	1965	12.5	1975	37.1	1985	31.6	1995	37.6	2005	4.9	2015	1.4
1946	-8.0	1956	6.5	1966	-10.0	1976	23.8	1986	18.6	1996	23.0	2006	15.8	2016	12.0
1947	5.6	1957	-10.7	1967	23.9	1977	-7.2	1987	5.2	1997	33.4	2007	5.5	2017	21.8
1948	5.4	1958	43.1	1968	11.0	1978	6.5	1988	16.6	1998	28.6	2008	-37.0	2018	-4.4

1941–1950: 14.3% | 1951–1960: 17.6% | 1961–1970: 9.0% | 1971–1980: 10.3% | 1981–1990: 14.6% | 1991–2000: 18.4% | 2001–2010: 3.6% | 2011–2018: 11.9%

World War II Begins • 1939	OPEC Oil Embargo • 1973	Peak of Technology Bubble • 2000
Pearl Harbor • 1941	Nixon Resigns • 1974	September 11th • 2001
		War in Iraq Begins • 2003
	Black Monday-Market Crash • 1987	
World War II Ends • 1945		Subprime Loan Issues Emerge • 2007
	Savings and Loan Crisis • 1989	
Korean War • 1950–1953		Global Credit Crisis Begins • 2008
	Gulf War • 1990–1991	
JFK Assassination • 1963	Asian Stock Market Crisis • 1997	"Great Recession" Declared Over • 2010

Sources: Morningstar Direct; Commonwealth Financial Network.

Past performance is no guarantee of future results. The information provided is for illustrative purposes and is not meant to represent the performance of any particular investment. It is not possible to invest directly in an index.

As you can see, despite big and even multiple single-year declines, investors who owned shares mirroring the S&P 500 across most ten-year periods saw their portfolios increase (assuming they reinvested the dividends). The key point, in terms of a contrarian approach, is that those increases were there within *a broad index.*

By *narrowing* the sectors assessed, analyzing companies to identify those that are undervalued, and prudently migrating capital to those most clearly poised for gains, it's a good bet that the returns within any of those ten-year periods could be markedly *higher*—and that those within *market cycles* could be better still.

Such careful analysis of opportunities, and close management of clients' investments, is exactly what I do—and have done—every day of my working life since 1985.

Still, people get scared

I won't pretend, however, that it's all I do. Part of my job is keeping people focused. Probably the worst moments of 2008 were the one-day crashes that occurred on consecutive Mondays, September 29 and October 6.

Then there was Black Monday in 1987.

I remember that during the first day of the crash some companies' stocks were trading with a ten-point spread between the bid and the ask. In today's markets, the spread between the bid and the ask is typically so tight it is fractional. But on Black Monday, the traders were inundated with sell orders and virtually no buyers. To me, it was a clear sign not to sell into this market. (I liken it to trying to sell your California house when a wildfire is in your backyard.)

I remember talking with a client's friend who had a very large position in AT&T stock. It was one of the few times I'd say, "Think about it. Do you really believe we're not going to use *telephones* after this? That your AT&T stock will be worthless?"

Pretty dispassionate, huh? And sure enough, the markets came back, just like electric utility stocks after Chernobyl.

That 1987 crash was the market's worst one-day crash ever—and it came back. The recovery happened far more quickly than many who lived through it seem to remember, covering the market's losses within a year and a half. In fact, I remember telling people later that same week, "Institutions are buying back their own shares." To me, it was an indicator of a good buying opportunity.

IBM and other blue-chip companies clearly believed their shares were undervalued and were scooping them up. Some companies were actually trading below their book values. In other words, these blue-chip companies were looking at *their own stock* and deciding that buying it back was a better investment than using these same funds to expand their businesses.

As the depth of the global financial crisis became clear, and with a presidential election looming, the Senate voted down a financial bailout bill and the market responded, shedding over 777 points in one day. Though a revised bill would pass two days later, a gloomy jobs report prompted another selloff—800 points—the following Monday.

Though my clients were worried, they knew after the first crash that they had a painstakingly structured plan in place, one designed to help meet their distribution needs. What they most wanted was someone to talk their friends off the ledge: relatives, neighbors, and colleagues who were scared to death. Many were thinking about selling off their blue-chip issues, worried there'd soon be blood in the streets.

* * *

The problem with the trend toward self-directed investing is that individual investors—to put it bluntly—are too easily frightened. I know that's a hugely unpopular point of view—with individual investors. Professional advisors, however, know the truth. We know because it walks through our doors and rings our phones every day, as people react on pure passion to the market's daily swings.

Still, the belief persists—fed by discount brokerages—that *anyone* can learn to make the market work to their advantage. Technically, it's true: anyone willing to train, to get accredited, and to study market cycles until they know them like the back of their hand *probably* can. But is that really how you want to spend your retirement? I'm guessing no.

And that's OK. It's why I'm here!

A dispassionate eye

I've been at this long enough to recognize immediately when a client fully comprehends the cyclical nature of markets: he no longer calls when one of his holdings drops.

That's what I call having a dispassionate eye. He or she may still be watching the market, but when the same client who, in the past, would have called the office on a really bad day doesn't so much as peep, I know they get it.

Let me be clear: there's nothing wrong with *watching* the markets. The risk lies in *reacting* to them. That's true whether the news on Wall Street is good or bad, because, as we've seen, the tendency of individual investors is to sell when their stocks are dropping and to buy when they're on the rise: the exact *opposite* of what they should do.

It's completely understandable, especially with retirees who are trying to protect their wealth. It is also unfortunate. It means that every day, people lose money for no good reason.

Wealthy people enjoy a distinct advantage over those still working to build wealth: the ability to hire someone—like me—to manage it.

My dispassionate eye allows me to confidently counter a concern I hear all the time, even from retirees who *understand* market cycles:

"I can't have stocks, because I don't have enough time to go through a bear market."

But here's the thing: most stock market declines have been intra-year. Keeping enough bonds and cash in your portfolio can help you ride it out. I'll cover this in relation to the strategies I enact on my clients' behalf in the next chapter. For now, page back a bit and look again at the first of the two charts in this one—specifically, at the line on that first chart labeled "bonds." I think you'll see what I mean: when the stock markets dropped, the bond markets held up pretty well.

The fallacy of timing the markets

Before we leave the subject of passion and its negative effects on investment performance, there's one last area we need to address: the absolute fallacy of securing your gains by timing the markets.

Before the crash of 1987, a very well-regarded economist's key economic indicators were sounding alarms. "The market is over-priced," she said.

Now, lots of people listen to this particular economist, with good reason. Her reputation is great and her assessments are usually spot-on. So, investors watched the market in anguish, wondering what would happen. But nothing did—until weeks after her comments. We had a one-day crash with the market losing 22 percent.

That economist never said, "It's going to go down 22 percent, and it's happening on this date." She only said, "The market is too high."

What is an individual investor supposed to do with that information? "When do I get out? When do I get back in?" You see, successfully timing the market relies on knowing the answer to both those questions.

A similar—yet very different—thing happened in '87 on the Friday prior to the Black Monday crash. You can still watch it on YouTube.

Asked for his postmortem on one of the market's worst weeks since the Great Depression, the late Martin Zweig, appearing on the PBS show *Wall $treet Week,* told host Louis Rukeyser, "I haven't been looking for a bear market per se ... I've been really, in my own mind, looking for a crash, but I didn't want to talk about it publicly because it's like shouting 'fire' in a crowded theater."

He might as well have done just that. The following Monday, the market took what remains, at this writing, its single largest percentage nosedive of all time.

But again: what was an individual investor supposed to do upon hearing that?

He could call his broker first thing Monday, I suppose—like hundreds of thousands of others—in the vain hope that he would somehow liquidate quicker than the institutional investors' computers were liquidating their holdings.

You see, on Sunday night, stocks began to sell off as markets opened in Asia and then in Europe. On Monday morning, the Dow fell at the open, as sell orders far outpaced buy orders. Big sell orders from institutional investors flooded in and continued throughout the day. Trading volume hit unprecedented levels, with share volume on the NYSE almost double the previous record (set the prior Friday).

My point: Even if you are doing everything you can in an effort to buy issues low and sell them high, you expose yourself to the same risks that those who wondered when the market would correct itself, in the first example, were taking. Stay in too long, and you risk a crash every bit as devastating to you, personally, as the second example was for thousands in October 1987.

The problem comes down to timing and investors' willingness to believe advisors who claim an ability to do it. Or worse, who think they can do it themselves. No one can on anything close to a consistent basis.

This is easy to see—when viewed through *dispassionate* eyes. Not, however, through the dollar signs that too often cloud the vision of investors when advisors regale them with stories of "beating the Street."

Think about what's required to actually *do* that on a regular basis. He must get it right not once, but twice. *Much more often than not.*

Still, we want to believe. "Somebody, somewhere," we think, "has to know when to get out!" Let me assure you: they don't.

I view those who rely on timing the market as broken clocks. Twice a day, they're right. But you only know *when* if there's a *working* clock nearby. What good is the broken one?

In every market environment, there will be purveyors of doom and gloom. There will also be advisors who promise to protect you from downturns in order to justify putting everything in equities. Both play on your passions, selling you on fear and hope, not reality.

We all know a crash or a correction is coming, sometime. But none of us knows *when*. We also know it's *possible* to time stock purchases and sales perfectly. It's just not *probable.* So which do you think is smarter: Trying to guess right, or managing your investments to mitigate risk?

*   *   *

This chapter has outlined the dangers of allowing passion to rule investment decisions. Getting caught up in the momentary swings of the market, at best, hinders investment appreciation. Significant growth is far more likely if we trust the market's cycles and dispassionately leverage them to our advantage.

Stock market corrections and bear markets have been temporary and, in time, have given way to the market's longer-term upward trend. That's why an approach that relies on careful analysis of company performance and migration of investment capital to underpriced issues can create real opportunities for building wealth—while attempting to time market highs and lows is a fool's errand.

Protection of assets is especially important to those nearing or already in retirement. Professional wealth advisors understand that proper diversification with a long-term focus is the best approach for getting clients through the highs and lows of the normal market and for softening the impact of protracted downturns. In part three, we'll see why.

Strategic Wealth Management

CHAPTER 7

Eliminate the Negative

A LOT HAS CHANGED in the financial services industry since I joined it over thirty-five years ago. Most of the changes have been for the better and form the bedrock of my approach to strategic wealth management.

For example, I trained as a stockbroker. No one calls themselves a broker anymore, me included. Today we're known by various names, from investment advisor to financial advisor to the term I use, because it best describes my job: wealth manager.

Back in the day, stockbrokers made their livings on commissions. They made money every time they bought or sold a security, which of course gave them an incentive to do both, thereby putting their needs (i.e., earnings) first. This longstanding, unbalanced compensation structure was (thankfully) replaced by fee-based investment advising, which puts the advisor on the same side as the client. The advisor is paid a percentage of the assets under management, assuring that both the client and advisor benefit if the assets grow in value.

This model creates a framework through which the advisor puts their clients' interests ahead of their own and would therefore be more likely to seek positive long-term results for both parties. Today, nearly all financial services are fee-based, and I think both the industry and investors are better off because of it.

The big mutual fund houses work differently now too. Many once assessed large up-front sales charges or back-end redemption fees and had much higher internal expense ratios than we typically see today. For example, 8 percent of the total being invested was commonly assessed, just to get into a fund. When that fee dropped to 5.75 percent, people thought it was a real steal.

Today, some funds have sales charges as low as 3.5 percent. And that's for people who still buy into the market that way—which the wealthy, in my experience, increasingly do not. It's now possible for individual investors to buy shares at *institutional rates,* as I will detail in the next chapter.

Another big change since I broke into the business is the advent of exchange traded funds (ETFs). The first, Standard and Poor's SPDR, began trading in 1993, more than a decade after I joined the industry.

While these and other changes have been fundamental and profound, a couple of things haven't changed: my interest in understanding clients' goals and my desire to help them get there.

This chapter and the next detail the approach to *strategic wealth management* I have honed and refined for more than thirty years.

Key considerations in seeking long-term prosperity

Potential traps can lay in wait along the path to a purpose-driven retirement. It's important to know what they are: their features, dangers, and some common misconceptions.

The foundation of the wealth management approach I customize for every client I serve is a concept I call strategic diversification. Investment gurus preach diversification all the time, but I believe not enough is said about the right kind of diversification. Is it enough to simply allocate your assets in different baskets? I don't think so. I believe it should be done in a way that permits the withdrawal, from income and growth on those assets, of the funds you'll need in order to enjoy the retirement you envision—without depleting the investment capital that produces future growth. I submit that, done properly, this approach offers the potential to grow wealth as retirement nears and throughout retirement.

At the core of this approach is *active management of the portfolio's investment allocation,* in order to draw retirement distribution needs using income from bonds, from dividends on equities and from investment growth. That income is provided by selectively trimming back positions in those asset classes that show higher performance in the current market cycle. (I'll get more deeply into the nuts and bolts of my approach in the next chapter.)

Active management is just what it sounds like: a lot of work. But it's what I believe best allows an advisor to have a tangible impact in a clients' investment portfolios, and I absolutely love doing it. I think that's because, as someone who grew up with the discomfort of not having enough money, I'm deeply motivated to help retirees live free of that concern. Developing and constantly fine-tuning my approach on my clients' behalves has brought me joy for over thirty years and helped my clients pursue their dreams.

There are, however, the aforementioned traps along the path, and they can cause problems if certain investments or investment products are not fully understood. Let's take some time to study three investments I often find in the accounts of retirees: *exchange traded funds, annuities,* and *structured products.*

Exchange traded funds

An ETF is a marketable security that tracks a stock index, bonds, or a basket of assets. Unlike mutual funds, ETFs trade like a common stock on a stock exchange and experience price changes throughout the trading day as they are bought and sold.

One of the most widely known and traded ETFs trades under the symbol SPDR (for "Standard & Poor's Depositary Receipts"). It tracks the S&P 500 Index, a market-value (a.k.a. market-capitalization) weighted index. The S&P 500 tracks the five hundred largest companies that are publicly traded in the US by market value and is the most common benchmark for the broader US equity markets. Put together by computers and traded using algorithms, funds like SPDR are the most popular types of ETF and have been since the SPDR fund debuted as the first, in 1993.

Most index-based ETFs are weighted by capitalizations (size) of the companies in the index they mirror. Stock in companies with the largest market caps carry the heaviest weighting—so, as those individual companies' stock prices increase, their weighting within the broader, multiple-company index on which the ETF is based increases too.

John W. Schoen, an award-winning online journalist, reported on CNBC.com on August 2, 2018, that "Apple had become the first-ever $1-trillion publicly listed US company, capping a decade-long rise in its stock price, fueled by its ubiquitous iPhone." Putting that into perspective, Schoen said Apple's market value was "greater than the combined market capitalization of ExxonMobil, Procter & Gamble, and AT&T, and now accounts for 4 percent of the S&P 500."

A few weeks before, Sean Williams, in a *Motley Fool* article titled "7 Fascinating Facts About the Broad-Based S&P 500," pointed out that the share values of the index's largest ten components (company stocks) account for more than 21 percent of the S&P 500's weighting. That means 2 percent of the companies in the S&P 500 index play a significant role in influencing the return on investments tied to the S&P. *Less* than 2 percent of them, in fact; the S&P tracks 500 companies, but some have issued more than one class of stock (i.e., components), and two of the stocks in the top ten as of the *Motley Fool* report were issued by the same company: Google (a.k.a. Alphabet).

A concentrated stock position can expose the investor to significant risk if bad news is reported on a company in which the investor holds a large position in that company's stock. Index ETFs and managers using active strategies can both expose assets to concentration risk. The difference is that *active* managers can choose at any time to sell off a portion or all of a stock holding.

Index ETFs, on the other hand, are *passively* managed, and the market-weighted construction most index ETFs use means that holdings only change as their capitalizations change. In an index ETF, a stock holding is not removed from the asset mix until it is removed from the index to which the ETF is tied. That, in turn, only happens when a company's revenues decline markedly, causing a drop in its stock price (and therefore a drop in its capitalization)—or when a company declares bankruptcy, which prompted, as one example, the Lehman Brothers removal from the S&P 500 Index.

The idiosyncratic methodologies used by index-based ETFs to select their baskets of securities—in a word, algorithms—can cause some other potential pitfalls: sector risk and style classification risk. Let's look at both.

Five of the previously discussed ten largest S&P holdings in mid-2018 were in the technology sector of the market. (I've already noted Google's two components; the other three were Apple, Microsoft, and Facebook.)

In addition to their status as *tech-sector* stocks, tech issues are also considered *growth-style* stocks.

So, it's fair to say that someone invested in the S&P 500 at the time was not only more concentrated in the technology sector but *also* weighted more in growth (more speculative) over value (less speculative) style stocks—*another* risk. What a deal, huh? It is important to understand the inherent structure of the index that an ETF tracks and the methodology the product employs.

In case you've forgotten how leading high-tech companies fell with the tech-bubble correction of 2000, let me remind you.

In the late '90s and the early part of 2000, the tech sector comprised a larger and larger percentage of the S&P 500, mainly because, as prices of technology stocks soared, so did their capitalizations—and their impact on the S&P 500.

Interestingly enough, in 2000, the Russell 1000 *Growth* Index was down over 22 percent for the year, while the Russell 1000 *Value* Index rose 7 percent. Can you see the importance of being familiar with the *type* of diversification your portfolio employs and how being diversified among sectors and styles can be prudent, even if investing in the same stock market?[5]

Market capitalization (cap) is a key component in the decisions about which issues will and will not be included in a given index. It is calculated by multiplying a company's outstanding shares by

---

5   Diversification does not assure a profit or protect against loss in declining markets, and diversification cannot guarantee that any objective or goal will be achieved.

the current market price of one share; the higher a stock's price, the higher the company's capitalization. When Apple hit $1 trillion in market cap, its stock was selling at its *all-time high price,* so anyone buying the S&P 500 index that day was also buying Apple *at that price.*

Now, I am not saying that stocks hitting their all-time highs means that they cannot continue to move higher. I just prefer to buy low whenever possible.

Unlike buying an ETF (passive) index, the manager of an active fund can choose to take some of their profits off the table when a stock of a particular style or sector is trading at or near its high and invest those profits elsewhere—for example, in companies that show consistent earnings growth but are not currently overvalued (i.e., overpriced).[6] Some people either don't understand this key fact or ignore it. Will Danoff's Fidelity Contrafund and the rising market value of Warren Buffett's Berkshire Hathaway are just two (albeit prominent) examples of active investing.

Let's look at another example of the important role active management can play by going back even further—to thirteen years before the first ETF debuted.

---

6   An actively managed fund relies on an investment manager attempting
     to meet an objective by actively choosing which investments to purchase,
     hold, and sell. These strategies often utilize in-depth analysis and methods
     to select investments which may involve more frequent trading resulting
     in higher portfolio turnover. This can increase trading costs and fees,
     lowering the overall returns of the portfolio as well as increase the possibil-
     ity of generating taxable capital gains. Active strategies are not suitable for
     all investors and there is no guarantee that any investing goal will be met.
     Investing involves risk including the loss of principal.

More on passive risk

In 1980, IBM and AT&T were the largest-cap companies in the S&P 500, and therefore held the two largest (most weighted) positions in that index. But by '89, Exxon and GE had pushed IBM to number three. All are huge companies, but just three years later—and a year before the S&P 500's SPDR was introduced—IBM was out of the top ten entirely. Yet if you'd mimicked what ETFs now achieve and invested in all the issues held in the S&P you'd have *still carried* IBM, though other issues were doing much better.

Fast-forward to 1998. Microsoft moved ahead of GE. Two years later, GE regained the top spot, reaching its all-time high, while Microsoft (thanks to the tech bubble's burst) fell to number seven. By 2009, GE was out of the top ten and falling fast—but everyone tracking the index *still owned some.*

> That's the active manager's goal: to prognosticate what's coming by constantly assessing every issue they own. Is it overvalued? Is there a problem here?

If this sounds like the *opposite* of active investment management, it is. An active manager, in this example, may have decided—looking at GE when it was at or near its all-time high—to either get out or at least pare back some of their GE position and move into Microsoft or another underpriced stock. That's the active manager's goal: to prognosticate what's coming by constantly assessing every issue they own. Is it overvalued? Is there a problem here?

News about the woes of GE's financial division had been coming out for months, and it was that division that eventually doomed the stock. Active managers could have gotten their assets out, but GE remained a key component of the by-then-introduced ETFs that were tracking the S&P.

It's analogous to the example of BP, which remained part of the mostly widely followed foreign index, MSCI's EAFE index, during the blowout of the Deepwater Horizon. But active managers could have sold BP and waited until the impacts of that catastrophe became clearer.

This isn't to say that active managers are infallible. These are, after all, very specific examples. One actively managed fund's manager is just as likely to choose incorrectly and misread signals as another is apt to get them right. However, I believe that, as with everything else in life, experience matters, and that an experienced active manager who has studied the markets' behavior for years and brings a systematic approach to managing client capital is more likely to make decisions that grow that capital, thereby offering more opportunities for growth than one would likely see by simply parking money in an index fund.

To me, at least, it's pretty obvious which approach offers more control and opportunity to manage risk. That's why active management can be compelling: having an actual, experienced, trained, intelligent person asking the tough questions. "Do I want to own this much General Electric right now? Or would I be better served to have more in Microsoft?" "Is it time to get out of IBM?"

Given these three key risks of ETFs (sector, style, and single-stock concentration risks) why are many financial advisors so enamored of them? Well, because the cost of running an ETF is cheap. ETFs do not have a staff of money managers and team of analysts to pay. The computer algorithm does all the work. But as we've seen, it bakes passivity into the cake.

Of course, acolytes of ETFs have arguments in favor of them, not least that active managers do not outperform their benchmark indices every year. But that can be a *function* of those managers' foresight, not the *result* of it.

Even Warren Buffett, perhaps the best investor of all time, has had many years in which he underperformed his benchmark index. Whether due to buying a stock early and waiting for the market to value it appropriately or the reverse effect on the back end (selling it before the broader market wakes up to its overvalued price), this comes with the active management turf.

In fact, if you look at Berkshire Hathaway's 2017 annual report, you'll see Buffett's track record from 1965 to 2017 shows he underperformed the S&P 500 nearly *one third* of the time. What is the difference between Buffett's active approach and one of passively waiting until a stock is totally played out or has even fallen out of an index? In this example, *over the same period,* his compounded annual gain was 20.9 percent, compared to the S&P's 9.9.

Active management done right (and when all the pieces fall into place) leverages buying low and selling high to a fare-thee-well. It is important to note, however, that not all active managers outperform passive ETFs. The parameters and strategies employed can vary greatly, and those strategies' efficacy is subject to the kinds of market forces at play. It is therefore important to understand the manager's investment strategy, process, and discipline.

It is also important to note that bond market ETFs are a whole different animal from equity ETFs. The general benefits of bond-related ETFs are that they offer low execution costs in acquiring a broad, diversified portfolio. The manager of an actively managed bond fund can make decisions regarding a specific holding's leverage and determine if such a position's expected return is outweighed by its risk—considerations which are not possible in index-based, equity ETFs.

In his research paper "Bonds are Different," Dr. James Moore, managing director and head of the investment solutions group at Pacific Investment Management Company, eloquently explains:

> Unlike equity indexes, where the market determines the weights, in bond indexes issuers principally determine the weights. With the exception of the Dow Jones Industrial Average, most commonly referenced equity benchmarks are capitalization weighted, with weights determined solely by the market capitalization of the company.
>
> Bond indexes are different. Weightings chiefly reflect how much debt a company or government issues, and the size of an individual security issued. Yet if a company issues more debt, the aggregate value of the enterprise is not fundamentally affected. Cash coming in is an asset; debt added is a liability. Ignoring issuance fees, the essential equation is: new cash in minus new debt owed equals zero.
>
> However, when a company *issues more debt,* its weight in a bond index increases. Why should an investor boost holdings in a company's liabilities because the company increases financial leverage?

It's a good question, to which I'll add: especially when *more* leverage can mean more risk?

I believe that portfolios shouldn't be solely constructed of ETFs. Depending on a client's circumstances, including equity ETFs in a portfolio could make sense. They may provide an offset against any years of underperformance that can occur when active managers are awaiting the market's awakening.

That said, investing purely in ETFs, or any static allocation for that matter, would make my life easier. I could trade hours of actively monitoring my client portfolios with time on the golf course or enjoying lunch with my friends. Neither compares, however, to the joy I get from working to meet and exceed my clients' expectations

I believe that the more educated one is, the better. One resource I have found helpful over the years is *Barron's*, which is published every weekend. It provides fact-based information and analysis dedicated to investing. Its columnists give readers insight into the thoughts, opinions, and market outlooks of some of the most respected and best minds on Wall Street. I consider Barron's to be a balanced, perceptive market analysis tool. If you are not currently reading it, I believe you should!

Annuities

People love hearing the word *guaranteed* when being offered an investment, and none are sold on the strength of that word more often than the next potential pitfall on the path to a purpose-driven retirement: annuities.

A couple of old adages spring to mind: if it sounds too good to be true, it probably is—even though those using egregious sales practices might tell you differently. But remember (old adage number two): nothing in this world is certain except death and (possibly) taxes.

Annuities tend to be restrictive, and certain kinds, like variable annuities, can have high annual costs. Generally, subject to some exceptions and conditions, these products should be held until age fifty-nine and a half. Withdrawals made prior to that are subject to a 10 percent IRS penalty, and surrender charges may also apply. Subject to some exceptions, they may also carry high redemption charges and back-end loads. The contingent deferred sales charge may be 10 percent in the first year and decrease from there by equal increments.

Let's say, for example, you buy an annuity at $100,000 with a 10-percent surrender schedule. If you decide you want to pull all your original investment out in the first year, you'll pay $10,000—to get *your own money* back. Redeem it during the second year and the charge drops to $9,000, and so on, until your purchase is fully vested ten years in. Even though you *paid in full* on day one. Every schedule is different; this is just one example. Currently, the average variable annuity surrender schedule is five to seven years (unless it's a bonus share class annuity, but those are becoming obsolete). Normally we only see a ten-year contract in the fixed-indexed (or fixed) annuity space. Clearly, liquidity is a very important consideration prior to buying an annuity.

Variable annuities may also have high annual fees and expenses. Their "guaranteed income benefits" generally *cost* you, the buyer, about 1 percent of the annuity's benefit base value per year—they are not offered for free, as some investors might assume.

Further, withdrawals of appreciated dollars, when taken after age fifty-nine and a half, are taxed at *ordinary income,* not capital gains, rates. The latter rates are levied on the appreciation of stocks and bonds and are much lower than income tax rates for people in the middle to top tax brackets. Of course, this depends on the sources of the money. Nonqualified money (contributions made with after-tax dollars) is taxed at an ordinary income rate to the extent of the gain in the contract. Qualified money, as alluded to earlier, is taxable at ordinary income levels. If a Roth is utilized, these will be tax free, subject to certain conditions.

Factoring in ordinary income tax costs is an important consideration before buying a variable annuity with after-tax money (a nonqualified annuity). It is also important to remember that beneficiaries of these annuities, when taking distributions, will have to pay ordinary income taxes on gains made on the *original* amount invested in the contract. They *cannot* take advantage of the stepped-up cost basis for inherited property currently available under US tax law. (The stepped-up cost basis rule allows the beneficiary to increase the basis to its fair market value on the owner's date of death.)

This is one example of why it's important to be sure of the structure, type of product, and associated costs. Annuity products run the gamut, from simple, single-premium immediate annuities (SPIAs) to variable annuities that access the markets and offer the tradeoff of increasing return potential by taking more risk.

At the SPIA end of this spectrum, the buyer pays a lump sum to an insurance company, which then pays the owner a steady stream of income for life or for a fixed period. These products generally come with lower internal rates of return but comparatively lower costs.

At the other end of the continuum, variable annuities give owners the option of taking on more risk for the possibility of earning a higher rate of return. These are generally more expensive compared to other types of annuity products. Across the annuity spectrum, fee structures, optional features, costs, and contract types vary significantly.

Variable annuities with a guarantee to double the benefit base ten years after purchase can be attractive to a fifty-five-year-old looking to retire at age sixty-five. Though it may carry a 10 percent surrender charge, he sees it as no problem, because he is hyperfocused on the seller's claim *guaranteeing to double its benefit base* at maturity, ten years after purchase. *That's a 7 percent increase per year*, he thinks. *Sounds great!* Especially if the stock market is struggling. "Geez," he tells himself, "I'm about to retire and can lock in a 7 percent yearly return!"

But let's look at things from the other side of the table.

In my opinion, annuities actuaries are interested in two numbers when formulating these products: the benefit guaranteed to the buyer and the actual *market value* of the annuity, i.e., the performance of its *underlying investments*.

Let's explore how potentially getting into the wrong product can have unintended consequences.

Let's consider a scenario where our fifty-five-year-old turns sixty-five. He originally invested $100,000, but *can't get* his $200,000 in a lump sum unless the market value of his underlying investments has *grown to $200,000.* In other words, if the underlying investments performed under 7 percent, our investor—in order to access the $200,000 benefit—must withdraw funds from the *guaranteed benefit account* incrementally over the reminder of his life, extending *further* the insurance company's access to *his* investment capital. Generally, annuities only allow a guaranteed income of a roughly 5 percent annual withdrawal for folks in our subject's age range. So, from his $200,000, he's limited to pulling out $10,000 a year. This is an example of a product being mismatched to the objectives of the client. This client may have been looking for accumulation but instead purchased a product designed to address income needs.

Let's go a step further.

If this same investor dies at age eighty and you calculate everything out—after he's paid all the expenses the company has mandated in the annuity agreement—the annualized return, on average, is just above 2.3 percent. The company that sold him the annuity has basically used *his* money to make *itself* a bunch more and returned a pittance in appreciation of the loan.

By the way, guaranteed income from an annuity is generally not adjusted for inflation. That can be problematic as the retiree's medical costs, housing expenses, and other living expenses increase over time. Though there are annuities that offer an inflation adjustment at an additional cost, I believe it is important to do a cost/benefit analysis to see if that option is worth the price.

Annuities too often sell based on investors' fears, leveraged by unscrupulous sales tactics warning of market uncertainty. Unfortunately, too many soon-to-be retirees hear the word *guarantee* and ask, "Where do I sign?" without considering all of the pros and cons of the product and whether it even makes sense for their portfolio and overall retirement strategy.

When you find yourself considering a vehicle that is marketed as a guaranteed anything—a hedge against market volatility, or against inflation, or against any other utterly unpredictable market force—remember: *no* company sells *any* product knowing it will lose money.

Purchasers of annuities must take the time to understand the many types and their associated costs. An advisor who works to the fiduciary standard can help determine which, if any, are suitable for the buyer's needs.

Annuities can make sense in certain cases. I believe, however, that for those with the risk tolerance and assets there can be more effective ways to protect and grow assets in retirement. As already noted, many annuities are restrictive and come with high surrender charges and tangible tax consequences for those in middle to top income tax brackets. An actively managed portfolio with similar objectives can provide more flexibility, potential for growth, and cost efficiency.

A possible case for using an annuity is an investor who wants a set amount of income during her lifetime, perhaps because she is concerned about outliving her savings during retirement. A SPIA could be especially suitable, particularly if she is unconcerned that her beneficiaries might receive a smaller inheritance.

The shorthand name for these insurance products is "immediate annuity." SPIAs tend not to be as popular among financial advisors who sell annuities, because they offer a much lower sales commission than deferred annuities.

With an immediate annuity, the investor makes a single, lump payment to an insurance company. The insurance company then pays a guaranteed stream of income. Immediate annuities generally start payments one month after purchase, and those payments continue either for as long as the annuitant (buyer) is alive or for a specified period of time. The longer the annuitant lives, the better their return will be, so immediate annuities are not for the investor in poor health—including the (literally) faint of heart.

You can help your purchase go further by adding a second person to the annuity (joint and survivor ownership), by guaranteeing that payments are made for a certain period, or by stipulating that the principal is fully refunded (refund annuity). Such provisions cost more, however, and payments are lower on jointly owned versions than on those taken out only on the life of the annuitant.

Once an immediate annuity's payments have commenced, there is no changing the terms. If something in your life changes and you need some of the principal you paid to purchase the annuity back, you're out of luck. The insurance company will only pay you on the schedule you set up under the terms of purchase. Neither will cancellation provide a refund of your principal. This can limit your ability to deal with an emergency situation or other crisis.

Getting a set fixed income (guaranteed by an insurance company) may sound great on the surface, but the internal rates of return on immediate annuities can be low when compared to competing investments. Keep in mind that the lower the interest rates at the time of locking in the immediate annuity payments, the lower the internal rate of return.

Even though annuities come with significant restrictions, barriers, and tradeoffs, they can make sense as part of a client's investment portfolio if they meet the client's objectives and investment goals—for instance, if the client's objective is tax-deferred growth or a greater degree of certainty of income. But it is important the client, before investing in any annuity, be fully aware that the tradeoff for this type of guarantee can be a lower potential rate of return—versus being in the markets—along with restrictions on accessing their principal and various tax consequences.

Structured products

If my strong opinions about annuities have left you feeling like they are the worst kind of distraction from the goal of protecting your wealth, not so fast. We haven't discussed the third threat to a purpose-driven retirement: structured products.

Just as insurance companies create and market annuities, banks and brokerage firms sell structured products, which include a myriad of complex conditions, yet come with certain assurances—like guarantees to principal and certain rates of return. The investor should carefully review the disclosure documents, as products of this nature include many stipulations and conditions in achieving these results.

The Securities and Exchange Commission's Rule 434 defines structured securities as "securities whose cash flow characteristics depend upon one or more indices or that have embedded forwards or options or securities where an investor's investment return and the issuer's payment obligations are contingent on, or highly sensitive to, changes in the value of underlying assets, indices, interest rates or cash flows."

Some structured products are built to limit exposure of capital to downside risk. This protection of principal is only valid if the product is held to maturity. Here's an example of how the underlying investment might look in a structured product with a five-year term.

For every $1,000 invested, the issuer uses a large portion of the investors' funds to buy a bond with enough interest-earning potential to grow to $1,000 by the end of the structured product's five-year term. The bond might cost $850 today and grow from bond interest paid during that five years to $1,000. With the leftover $150 of the investor's outlay, the issuer purchases the derivatives (usually options) of an underlying asset needed to produce whatever the investment strategy requires. So a structured product's return is linked to the performance of an *underlying* asset, such as an index, or "basket" of securities.

The disadvantages of structured products may include:

- ***Limited appreciation potential.*** Issuers of structured products can (and usually do) set a cap on the maximum value at maturity.

- ***Credit risk.*** Structured products are unsecured debt, therefore investors are subject to the default risk and credit risk of the issuer.

- ***Lack of liquidity.*** After their initial offering, structured products trade infrequently and are primarily traded on an over-the-counter market. The brokerage firm or investment bank issuers of the product are not obligated to provide bids in this market. If an investor sells a structured product prior to term maturity, the value is determined by what a buyer is willing to pay at that time, which may be considerably less than the principal invested. Generally, illiquid markets are not favorable to sellers.

- **Highly complicated return calculations.** The calculation methodologies may vary significantly from product to product. This complexity makes it difficult to determine how the structured product would perform in comparison to simply owning the underlying asset.

- **Lack of transparency of expenses.** Some structured product issuers work their pricing costs into their derivative models to hide the expense to the investor. This makes it hard for the investor to compare the costs of different issuers of similar structured products.

Structured products tend to have at least a five-year holding period. They come with certain assurances—like guarantees to principal and certain rates of return—but they can also cap your *appreciation.* For example, a 10-percent cap (annually) means that even when the bulls are running and your portfolio is up 15 percent, you'll get 10 percent on this product. You'll also sacrifice any dividends and interest above that cap.

Remember the last chapter's discussion of market cycles? It's a lot easier for the firm to win when they know they'll have a full cycle—better yet, two. And that's why seven- and ten-year commitments are even more common than five-year terms.

So why, when supposedly investing in the stock market, would anyone agree to make their assets illiquid? Again: fear. The (here comes that word) guarantee of not losing money. It's just that, with structured products, you're guaranteed to give up some of the upside, as well.

Further, structured products' guarantee against downside risk isn't what it seems, because sometimes the firms selling them are the ones *backing* them. Let me explain.

"Principal-protected" products are not always insured by the Federal Deposit Insurance Corporation in the United States; they may only be insured by the issuer and thus could potentially lose the principal if there is a liquidity crisis or bankruptcy. Put simply, if the company that sold you the product goes belly-up, you could lose it all or, if lucky, get pennies on your dollars—just ask those who owned structured products from Lehman Brothers in 2008.

As I said earlier, be sure to carefully review the conditions and disclosures of the structured product before deciding to invest. Products of this nature include many stipulations and conditions in achieving their rates of return, and the calculation methodologies may vary significantly from product to product.

* * *

People want peace of mind. Who can blame them? But these three potential traps along the path to retirement must be carefully evaluated and considered. We must not be so focused on guarantees that we lull ourselves into a false sense of security. Real security is the objective, and that only results from a thorough knowledge of what you are investing in and why. A financial advisor who works to the fiduciary standard can help you determine if and when these products make sense for inclusion in your portfolio, based on your objectives.

> Without an advisor working in your best interests, you can be more susceptible to pitfalls that don't merely limit the power of your wealth but can substantially diminish it.

And these are the tip of the iceberg. There are countless opportunities out there for losing—or at least not getting the best return on—your money, and wealth doesn't render you immune to them. Without an advisor working in your best interests, you can be more susceptible to pitfalls that don't merely limit the power of your wealth but can substantially diminish it. And who wants that?

In chapter 8, I'll turn to what every investor *does* want, with a look at the three key tenets I apply in working to protect, enhance, and extend the power of my clients' wealth.

Accentuate the Positive

THROUGHOUT THIS BOOK, I've talked about my bottom-line orientation. I expect clients to judge me on the same standard I apply to myself. Getting you the best risk/reward ratio on your investments is my lone priority.

My ability to do that is directly proportional to my familiarity with your circumstances and goals. In chapter 5, you considered what peace of mind looks like for you and began thinking about what—beyond a basic sense of ease around your finances and your survivors' security—your Act Two of retirement looks like.

Getting a clear picture of that is critical. Without it, retirement can quickly become an endless string of empty hours, which become days, weeks, months, and years.

The success you attained in your working life was hard-won. You *absolutely* deserve all the downtime you like, whenever you want to enjoy it. But the thought of retirement makes it easy to forget that success in any endeavor—*retirement included*—relies on clear goals and plans for achieving them.

Companies tend to attract customers who share their values. Mine is no exception. The huge majority of my clients relish the opportunity to put their expertise to work in retirement in another pursuit they are passionate about.

In this chapter, I share three key elements of the approach I take to *strategic wealth management* on behalf of my clients. As you read, I encourage you to stop occasionally to consider what you'd still like to accomplish. Think about how your fiscal resources can make that possible. Consider, too, the *nonfiscal* legacy you want your work in retirement to leave. Don't worry about getting specific just yet; we'll pin down the particulars in chapter 9.

For now, let's focus on the fiscal side, with a look at my:

Three pillars of strategic wealth management

We've discussed how fear too often drives individual investors' decisions: they sell when an issue is falling (fear of further losses); buy when a stock is already near its peak (fear of missing out); or fail to think about how a particular product or investment might affect their retirement strategy or portfolio *before* purchasing it (fear of doing nothing).[7]

In my thirty-plus years as an advisor, I've come to believe that, in protecting and growing wealth, nothing is more important than investing in a diversified portfolio. This is one that includes many different asset classes and is actively managed by an advisor who keeps enough holdings in bonds and cash to get through the stock markets' inevitable downward trends.

Still, fear is not a light switch, something easily turned off. So especially with new clients, I spend a lot of time helping them focus

---

7   No diversification or allocation strategy can assure that any objective or goal will be achieved. All investments are subject to risk of principal

beyond their fears by sharing the information and experience I now share with you.

The strategic managing of my clients' wealth rests on three pillars: **real diversity of investments, a safety net of bonds and cash**, and **buying on weakness and selling on strength.** Like the analogy of the three-legged stool, each pillar is critical in making the plans I enact for clients stand up, in terms of protecting and increasing wealth. Omit or even neglect any one and the strategy can't succeed.

Pillar One: Real diversity of investments

Lots of advisors talk about the importance of diversifying your holdings, but what does that mean? Advisors who focus on buying and selling stocks might say it means having a good mix of value stocks and growth stocks. Or they may preach diversification across market sectors: a combination, say, of tech, financial, and energy stocks. And as far as they go, they're right.

Bond marketeers may tell you to diversify across government, corporate, mortgage-backed, and municipal bonds.

You may even find those selling structured products and annuities, covered in the previous chapter, encouraging you to buy *several different kinds* of these products!

Real diversification, however, means a mix of holdings *that make sense for your particular situation.* This often means choosing properly allocated combinations of large-, mid-, and small-cap domestic and foreign equities for long-term growth; bonds for potential income; and liquid assets—such as money markets, cash, and short-term treasuries—to meet more immediate expenses and income needs.

These three—equities, bonds, and liquid assets—are exactly the asset classes I focus most upon.

These three—equities, bonds, and liquid assets—are exactly the asset classes I focus *most* upon. My experience has convinced me that they can provide the most diversity when designing portfolios to help protect, grow, and distribute the wealth my clients will count on for their purpose-driven retirements—and for the fiscal legacies (the estates) they'll leave behind.

One of these *three main asset classes* offers real opportunity for growth: equities. Bonds offer higher yields than money markets, but fluctuate in value. Cash, meanwhile, only fluctuates in *relative* value (i.e., in the marketplace; its greatest strength is its stability).

Within the two more volatile of these three main asset classes— equities and bonds—lies a whole galaxy of more specific asset classes. This chart shows how certain types of them performed over a three volatile time periods: the technology bubble of 2000, the terrorist attacks of September 11th, 2001, and the beginning of the war in Iraq in 2003.

Asset Class Returns
Annual Returns for Key Indices (2000-2003) Ranked in order of performance (Best to Worst)

2000	2001	2002	2003
22.83% Small Cap Value	14.02% Small Cap Value	10.25% Core Fixed Income	56.28% Emerging Markets
11.63% Core Fixed Income	8.44% Core Fixed Income	-6.00% Emerging Markets	48.54% Small Cap Growth
7.01% Large Cap Value	-2.38% Emerging Markets	-9.80% Diversified Portfolio	46.03% Small Cap Value
-1.1% Diversified Portfolio	-4.80% Diversified Portfolio	-11.43% Small Cap Value	39.17% International Equity
-7.79% Large Cap Core	-5.60% Large Cap Value	-15.52% Large Cap Value	30.03% Large Cap Value
-13.96% International Equity	-9.23% Small Cap Growth	-15.66% International Equity	29.89% Large Cap Core
-22.42% Large Cap Growth	-12.45% Large Cap Core	-21.65% Large Cap Core	29.75% Large Cap Growth
-22.43% Small Cap Growth	-20.42% Large Cap Growth	-27.88% Large Cap Growth	23.50% Diversified Portfolio
-30.61% Emerging Markets	-21.21% International Equity	-30.26% Small Cap Growth	4.11% Core Fixed Income

Large Cap Value = Russell® 1000 Value Index

Small Cap Value = Russell® 2000 Value Index

Small Cap Growth = Russell® 2000 Growth Index

Large Cap Core = Russell® 1000 Index

Emerging Markets = MSCI Emerging Markets Index

Large Cap Growth = Russell® 1000 Growth Index

International Equity = MSCI EAFE Index

Core Fixed Income = Bloomberg Barclays U.S. Aggregate Bond Index

Diversified Portfolio = Diversified Portfolio is composed of 35% Barclays US Aggregate Bond Index, 10% MSCI EAFE Index, 10% Russell 2000 Index, 22.5% Russell 1000 Growth Index and 22.5% Russell 1000 Value Index

Past performance is no guarantee of future results. The information provided is for illustrative purposes and is not meant to represent the performance of any particular investment. It is not possible to invest directly in an index. Sources: Morningstar Direct; Commonwealth Financial Network.

Let's begin breaking down this information in the year 2000, when the tech-bubble burst. *Value* stocks and core fixed income issues (bonds) did just fine, while *growth* stocks got killed. Even a portfolio diversified to a 60-percent equity/40-percent bond ratio had a negative return. (As noted earlier, *value* stocks are those considered underpriced, waiting for the markets to realize their value. They may have higher dividend payout ratios or low financial ratios such as price-to-book or price-earnings. Investors purchase them in anticipation of appreciation, if and when it happens. *Growth* stocks, meanwhile, are those priced in line with their companies' successful track records and have substantial potential for growth in the foreseeable future. Growth companies often devote most of their current revenue toward further expansion. Their stocks tend to be considered expensive when compared to value stocks, but their success indicates continued growth, which is why investors buy them.)

So in looking at the 2000 tech-bubble burst, and doing so in the context of drawing retirement distribution needs, retirees with a diversified portfolio—and by that I mean one not just tied to the broad S&P 500 Index—could have taken their distributions from their value stocks and bonds and done just fine. The tech bubble hit growth stocks, which comprised a disproportionate percentage of the S&P (which, as we have seen, growth stocks tend to do)—versus what a truly diversified portfolio would include.

In 2001, you could still sell from the asset classes of small-cap value stocks and "core fixed income" issues (domestic bonds) at a profit, but by 2002, both value and growth indexes were down. You'd instead take your distribution needs from bonds. Conceptually, then, this three-year period—one of the worst ever for growth stocks—could have been navigated through true diversification. In '03, '04, '05, and '06, all the equities indexes were back, and back strong.

We've discussed market cycles, but here's the thing: you never know when they're going to change. At my website (Debrabrede.com) you'll find a chart that shows asset class returns from 1999–2018, and I hope you'll take a moment to check it out. It covers several market cycles and really brings home the difficulty of predicting when a cycle will change. Simply follow any one asset class throughout the whole chart—long-term bonds, large-cap core, whatever you like—and you'll see that there are years when it's down near the bottom and others that it's near the top. The takeaway: *there are no set patterns in asset class movements.*

This beautifully illustrates why the one-size-fits-all approach—for example, balanced funds (60 percent equities/40 percent bonds) or target date funds (comprised of equities and bonds, but weighted more toward bonds as the investor ages), things many people hold in their 401s or IRAs—may not grow wealth over time. I have found that a portfolio holding different asset classes, separated out to allow for distributions on strength from one asset class over another as market cycles change, offers what I believe to be greater opportunities for doing so.

Wealth is more quickly diminished when retirement distributions are drawn from a balanced fund or target date fund during a down period in the stock markets. In a balanced fund comprised of 60 percent equities and 40 percent bonds, 60 percent of the distribution is taken from equities, even if the stock market is down. With an advisor that is actively managing the portfolio allocation, the client benefits from the advisor's ability to properly rebalance and take appropriate strategic distributions. Allow me to further illustrate.

Say you're holding an IRA in a balanced fund with that classic 60 percent stocks/40 percent bonds mix. When you take, say, a $10,000 distribution from that fund, $6,000 comes from the stock side and

$4,000 from the bond stake. In 2002, those in balanced funds were taking the *majority* of their distributions from the *weakest place: stocks.* As the last chart shows, the diversified portfolio was *down* 9.8 percent. Those taking distributions from such portfolios made what could have been a loss on paper an *actual* loss! Compare that with individuals who were able to take distributions from bond holdings.

I see it all the time: financial services companies doing distributions across all of a client's holdings on a straight-percentage basis. If you're 40 percent in large-cap growth, 10 in small- and mid-cap, 10 percent in international equity, and the rest in bonds, they base your distribution on that allocation instead of *leveraging the strengths* in the market and *avoiding* its weaknesses. The result: that investor may not do as well over time.

By having your holdings in separate and different asset classes and drawing from strength—taking distributions using active allocation management—you let the market go through its cycle. But it takes a ton of work. My last three months of every year are grueling. I spend hours with my staff, analyzing where we'll take distributions for clients to assure we have properly managed their required distributions for the year and rebalancing their accounts.

Of course, people don't always take only the distribution amounts we determined in our planning when the year turns. Just yesterday, a retired client called out of a clear blue sky: "I'm buying my daughter a car; can you send me forty grand?"

So I looked at the client's portfolio and said, "OK, no problem. Small cap is up right now, we're going to take it from there." Take that same money from a balanced fund or proportionately from all their holdings, and you've just diminished the client's earning power—simply because you haven't based the distribution on the performance of the asset classes they hold.

In 2016, international markets were the worst-performing

equity class, and many individuals would have naturally preferred to take their distribution from their international holdings—not their value equities, which were up in price. But international markets offered a buying opportunity, not a selling opportunity, given market circumstances. Inherently then—and contrary to investor senti-ments—it made sense to add to international holdings as part of a diversified portfolio's equity allocation.

Hopefully you don't need another at this point, but this is an example of the risks in allowing fear to drive investment decisions.

Investors who sold from their international equities in 2016 would have given up on an asset class that was up just 1.5 percent. If a distribution was needed, it may have been much better to take it from small-cap value, which moved up 31.7 percent. (Of course, a larger capital gain in a nonretirement account means more tax. But as I know from experience, investors prefer gains to losses. So for me, worrying inordinately about the possibility of taxes on gains is kind of like refusing a bonus at work because you'll have to give some of it to Uncle Sam.)

Those that added to or at least did not sell their international holdings benefited by the MSCI EAFE Index returning 25.6 percent in 2017. Those invested in small-cap value saw the Russell 2000 Value Index return only 7.8 percent that year.

So Pillar 1 of my approach to strategic wealth management is real diversification. It's something which is hard to actualize, but a task I am only too happy to take on for my clients' benefit.

Pillar Two: A safety net of bonds and cash

There is a particular market phenomenon by which those who lack a trusted advisor can get thrown off track: intra-year declines. Another chart can help with understanding them, and why fear of them is the wrong response:

Annual returns and intra-year declines

S&P 500 intra-year declines vs. calendar year returns
Despite average intra-year drops of 13.9%, annual returns positive in 29 of 39 years

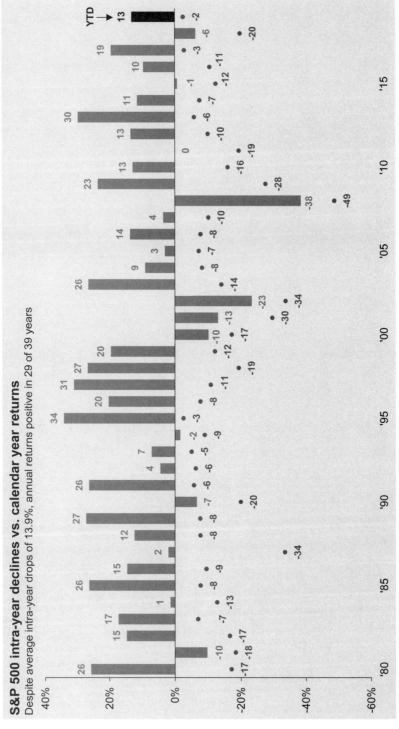

Source: FactSet, Standard & Poor's, J.P. Morgan Asset Management.
Returns are based on price index only and do not include dividends. Intra-year drops refers to the largest market drops from a peak to a trough during the year. For illustrative purposes only. Returns shown are calendar year returns from 1980 to 2018, over which time period the average annual return was 8.4%.
Guide to the Markets – U.S. Data are as of March 31, 2019.

J.P.Morgan
Asset Management

As the chart shows, while the stock market increases in value most years, it is also the case that at some point in nearly every year the stock market experiences a significant decline in value: an "intra-year" decline.

Take, for example, 2016. My team and I had just completed our usual three months of hard labor at the end of 2015 positioning clients' accounts to cover their distributions for the coming year. We had just rebalanced accounts only to see the S&P 500 steeply decline in January 2016 by about 11 percent—in just one month! The market stayed down in February.

Many individuals take their required minimum distributions (RMDs) from their retirement accounts in January or February of each year and use that money to help cover their living expenses all year long. These folks were looking at steep losses in their equity holdings at the very time they needed to withdraw from their accounts. We were in the midst of a storm.

The rest of the story is familiar: some people wanted to get out. People were calling me: "My God, will the markets go lower?" Well, no one really knew because markets do not move just on fundamentals, but also on the principles of behavioral finance.

Of course, I wasn't going to sell from their equities to cover their RMDs. I had already done the planning ahead of time, before the storm hit, and these clients had plenty of stable assets to take from without being forced to sell from their equities in the midst of a sharp downturn.

As the chart shows, by the end of 2016, the losses in January and February of that year were merely a ripple. The S&P 500 closed up 10 percent, a huge swing in an intra-year period. By taking from their bonds to cover the January and February RMDs, we positioned these clients' equity holdings to benefit from this rebound in the stock market.

Look at 2010. The market was down 16 percent intra-year and up 13 by the end. And how about that 19 percent drop in 2011?

When the 2011 drop started, I was actually in India at an orphanage where I volunteer (and which I'll talk about a bit later in the book). You can't really get the internet at the orphanage, but we went into the city to get supplies and as I hit up my smartphone, I saw that the equity markets were reacting badly to some news.

The S&P's rating agency had downgraded US Treasury bonds from AAA to AA in the midst of a congressional harangue over the country's debt ceiling. News media coverage painted worst-case scenarios, of course: people not getting their social security checks, government workers not getting paid, all kinds of politically driven nonsense.

Halfway around the world from me, in Boston, it was the middle of the night. But I knew what my staff would face in the morning with stock markets going down, so I sent an email.

"When people call, tell them not to sell their equity positions, this is craziness," I wrote. "Downgrade of treasuries should affect the treasury market, not the stock market."

That's because when a bond is downgraded, the issuer usually will need to pay more in interest to entice buyers. The S&P's "historic" downgrade was from outstanding to (merely!) excellent. For these reasons, I believed this crisis was no crisis at all. If anything, I believed it was an opportunity to buy equities—not sell them.

But it wasn't treasury bonds that would suffer, it was stocks, as self-directed investors did what they often do: overreact.

When rationality returned, people saw that it all meant nothing: Our treasury is solid, the government could always raise money through taxes—and voilà, the market rebounded by year's end. But think of those people who sold out when it was down!

Intra-year declines like these scare the daylights out of people who manage their own wealth but historically they have proved to be temporary. They are also a prime reason for keeping enough capital *outside* of the equity markets—in bonds and cash—to cover income needs for at least four to five years.

"But if intra-year declines are temporary," you may be wondering, "why do I need four to five years' worth of income outside the stock market?"

Two reasons: bear markets and emergencies.

Let me be clear: bear markets don't remove good investment opportunities. On the contrary, I believe they expand them. Still, you're likely to wait for substantial appreciation while the broader economy is hurting. Without a few years of your distribution needs in nonequity holdings such as bonds and cash, you'll be forced to sell off equities while they are down—and more importantly, the capital (read: wealth) you bought them with.

As we have seen, bear markets signal the midpoint of each market cycle, and typically, market cycles, looking back, have run four to five years. So keeping liquid funds sufficient to see you through a *complete* cycle will help you protect your investment capital.

Whatever the markets are doing, other events can sap capital.

Maybe you're still working. What if you lose your job? C-level positions can take a year, sometimes more, to replace. And if you're in retirement, your savings *are* your income. When the markets turn bear—we know they *will*, we just don't know *when*—you'll again want to draw upon liquid assets, so your capital in equities can ride out the markets' malaise.

I also see people get hurt when their kids need help. Maybe a son loses his job, and his retired parents have to step up to the plate.

A reserve of four to five years in nonequity investments is your safety net. Depending on your circumstances, more may be even better, because we never know what's going to happen in life. You don't want to overcompensate (remember my client who keeps a million in cash at all times?), but what looks like overcompensation to one person is peace of mind to someone else.

Whatever peace of mind is for you, putting in place a reserve of nonequity investments can help you to confidently remain invested in equities over the long haul. That lets my final pillar of strategic wealth management play its role of building wealth via your investment portfolio.

Pillar Three: Buy on weakness, sell on strength

In the last chapter, in discussing ETFs, I noted how the top companies in the S&P 500 Index are often on the higher end of their share values. If they weren't, they wouldn't be in the top ten, right? So, when you buy an ETF that's tied to an index, you are buying *not* on weakness but on the strength of the highest-weighted stocks in that index.

The same goes for selling low. When a stock you own is falling but its fundamentals are strong, selling is the opposite of what you should do. That, as we've seen, is a *buying* opportunity. But just as important as *when* you buy or sell is *how* you do. This is where active management is important.

In the last chapter, I discussed the huge decline, over the course of my career, in the sales fees and redemption charges assessed to individual investors on actively-managed mutual funds, from as much as 8 percent back in the day to as low as 3.5 percent now.

What if you could lower the costs associated with those investments *even further*? You can by investing in the institutional share class of an actively managed mutual fund.

On Wall Street, big institutions buy in big quantities and receive more favorable pricing based on that volume. Think of it this way: when McDonald's buys tons of ketchup for their thousands of stores, their price per ounce is extremely low compared to what you or I pay at the grocery store. McDonald's pays the wholesale, "institutional" price.

Mutual funds offer the equivalent of wholesale pricing through their "institutional" share class, often designated as I-shares, vs. retail A- and C-shares. For example, I-shares typically have expense ratios around 1 percent less than retail (C) shares. This is because C-shares carry what's called a 12b-1 fee, where the I-shares do not. 12b-1 fees cover a fund's advertising and marketing costs, including commissions paid to the marketers—financial advisors—for recommending the funds to their clients.

Another option for retail investors who are purchasing outside of an advisory agreement is to invest in A-shares. Though this class does charge investors an up-front commission (also known as a front-end sales load), most A-share sales loads are about 5.75 percent (though some go as high as 8.5 percent) and many also carry a 12b-1 fee. Holding A-shares for a longer period of time in a brokerage account can represent a lower-cost alternative to C-shares. (Remember, always read the fund prospectus before making any investment.)

Neither I- nor C-shares typically carry up-front sale charges, yet it is common to see an *additional* 1 percent redemption charge imposed on C-share investors who don't stay in the given fund's family for at least one year. But I-share investors typically see no such charges or time constraints.

Through my broker/dealer,[8] I am able to offer the I-share class of mutual funds to my advisory clients. This lets me give individual (a.k.a. retail) investors like you pricing that was previously available only to large institutions (or through some 401(k) plans).

The upshot: retail investors no longer need huge sums of money to get into the same funds that big institutions are buying. Coupled with an advisor who understands her client's goals, this wider access gives individual investors options for diversification—and for implementing highly strategic approaches to wealth management—that they never had back when I started in this business.

What I love most about being able to place a client in the I-share class of mutual funds is that, depending on the makeup of their portfolio as a whole, the savings over the expense of C-class shares can potentially *offset the cost of the investment advisory fee.*

In other words, if the client took the do-it-yourself approach—doing all the work of researching and finding the fund, monitoring, and rebalancing as needed—what they'd pay in 12b-1 expenses on C-class shares *can* cover the cost of hiring me, of paying my investment advisory fee, and of my investing the same amount of capital in I-shares.

---

8   An RIA (Registered Investment Adviser) broker/dealer is a company that registered investment professionals like me must affiliate with in order to buy and sell investment products on behalf of investors. The SEC (Securities and Exchange Commission) regulates both broker/dealers and investment advisors. While the SEC maintains the direct responsibility to oversee SEC-registered investment advisers, it delegates the supervision of broker/dealers and their financial advisors to FINRA. FINRA, in turn, requires all broker/dealers and their financial advisors to register with FINRA for supervision purposes. In addition to that, each of the individual states requires all broker/dealers and financial advisors who solicit or transact business within that jurisdiction to register with the state as well. Mine is RIA-Commonwealth Financial Network.

Whether you're invested in A- or C-shares, it's smart to have a conversation with your financial advisor. The savings on internal expenses with I-shares, compared to the cost of C- *and* A-class shares, can offset the cost of coming to a *process-driven wealth manager* like me, even with my fee factored in. And by leveraging that expertise, you'll save time and effort of undertaking the whole separate education required to fully understand the finer points of regularly, and more important wisely, rebalancing your accounts.

Think of *active portfolio management* as tending a garden. When a plant has matured, flowered, and given you joy, but is now overgrown, it's time to cut it back so other plants in your garden can prosper. Active portfolio management does just that. It recognizes when an investment is at a place to take profits and move into an issue that's poised for growth.

All of which is much easier said than done. Especially when their retirement savings are on the line, fiscal crises can easily convince self-directed investors that they're about to lose everything, to believe the extremely reliable behavior of the market is gone forever, never to return.

But it always does. The only question is *when*.

The three pillars of my wealth management strategy address that question. By adhering to them and doing the full-time work they require, I help ensure my clients have places from which to draw their distribution needs, whether during steep intra-year market declines, longer-term bear markets, or emergency situations. All the while, I'm also actively managing their portfolios to help grow their wealth.

So, what will you do with your wealth? Let's find out. Your purpose-driven retirement awaits, in chapter 9.

Part Four

Giving Back

Purpose-Driven Retirement

PEACE OF MIND is a powerful force. Knowing that we and those closest to us are secure allows us to focus our attention on other things—sometimes to our detriment.

Our drive to always improve our situations is a bedrock concept of Keynesian economics known as *induced consumption.* It connects our spending habits to the availability of disposable income. We can illustrate the concept with a simple example.

A man stops at a gas station to fill up. Doing so assures he'll have enough fuel to get to and from work for the rest of the week. He has enough money in his pocket to buy the gas and to meet his other expenses until he gets his next paycheck, with a bit to spare.

He sees an ad on the pump: a premium car wash for three dollars with a purchase of ten gallons or more. A car wash was the furthest thing from his mind when he pulled in, but the next thing he knows, he's looking at his car. "It is pretty dirty," he reasons, "and I'll be saving money to boot!"

He won't, of course; if he were *saving* money he'd head to his bank's drive-through window and deposit those three bucks.

Who hasn't done this same thing? I know I have. If I had a share of Apple stock for every time I've stopped for one shirt at my favorite discount store only to walk out with two or three—and then to hear my husband, Ken laugh as I told him how much money I saved—well, I'd own a bushel of APPL.

I'm not making a value judgment here. Our tendency to expend discretionary income is neither good nor bad. It just is. But what if we committed to spending it *with a purpose*?

One advantage of wealth is that *we can*.

It only takes a clear picture of what matters most to you and figuring out the best way to achieve the impact you want to make. That may not involve spending money at all. You might spend *time*—with your grandchildren or mentoring underprivileged kids. You might *donate* physical resources you no longer need to a local shelter.

Discretionary spending can take many forms, but one constant holds: the more confident you are of your security in retirement, the easier it becomes to do the *extra* things you've always wanted to do, whether they benefit you, family, friends, a favorite cause, or a total stranger.

In chapter 5, you considered questions to define what peace of mind means to you. We've since seen how the reliability of market cycles, combined with my three-pillared, strategic approach to wealth management, helps leverage those cycles to create a fiscal safety net for you and yours, and *income and growth* in retirement, so you can pursue whatever purpose-driven retirement means to you.

This chapter poses questions to help you figure that out. But before you consider them, it's important to reiterate a point made earlier in the book: **"I don't want to do *anything* in retirement!"**

I hear this all the time, but it still surprises me.

Maybe it's because I'm not one to let the proverbial grass grow under her feet. Perhaps it's because the soon-to-be retirees I hear it from are extremely successful people. They've achieved success and wealth through constant work, and it seems obvious that they'd succeed in doing nothing for—oh, fifteen or twenty minutes.

I understand the sentiment, don't get me wrong. Who isn't at least tempted by the idea of finding a deserted beach and soaking up the sun and surf for months, to put themselves right after years of responsibility and the constant critical thinking that comes with it?

But even if they lazed oceanside (or mountaintop) for six months or a year, or played golf, or tennis—or even sat in a tiki bar each day with instructions to the staff that each empty Bahama mama constituted an order for another—it wouldn't last. I know, because I've seen these and many similar retirement plans fail. Successful people are active people.

Successful retirement, therefore, is about more than having enough money to live comfortably for the rest of your life. It requires a *sense of purpose,* a meaningful activity that connects you with something bigger than yourself. The following questions and observations can help you find purpose that makes your postwork life as enriching in intangible ways as your career has been in the more tangible sense.

As you read through these questions, do so as if you are starting a whole new life. Because you are.

The basics

Where do you want to live?

What family members or friends do you want nearby?

Annnnnd ... that's it for the basics!

The heavies (in no particular order)

What personal passions do you want to pursue with your time in retirement?

What are you going to do all day long?

What breaks your heart when you see it? Is it orphans, starving children, families without homes, crippled children, abused women, abandoned animals, polluted beaches?

What makes you feel good? Take a meal to an elderly neighbor. Mentor a fatherless or motherless child, build a house with Habitat for Humanity. I loved, and have many clients who loved, that experience.

What might you do to make a difference in someone else's life? On an early trip to India, I caught one of the orphan boys copying another student's homework before class. I called him out on this cheating and told him that getting a good education would allow him to get a good job one day and ensure he would not live in poverty. I strongly emphasized that he could learn nothing by cheating. At the time, I was wearing a Harvard Business School cap, which I promptly took off my own head and put on his. I said, "Someday I want to see you go to Harvard, and I will help pay your tuition." He didn't know anything about Harvard but loved the hat—I saw it on his head every day after that. Over the next year, he moved to the top of his class. It was a small thing to me at the time. But not to him.

Are you more comfortable handing a *check* to your favorite charity or giving your *time* to that same cause? Truth be told, I would probably prefer writing a check to the orphanage I've mentioned; India is no short trip, and I go every year. But as the old saying goes, children need your presence more than your presents.

By physically making a trip to this same orphanage in India each year, I see the children's needs firsthand. During my first visit, I noticed that the only transportation the orphanage had to take the kids to and from school were a van and a Jeep (which doubled as an ambulance, to transport any sick kids). This meant that the older kids often had to wait a very long time for their transport home from school. My next big donation was a school bus.

These yearly trips have allowed me, my husband, and our daughter and son to connect more deeply with the orphans. During the course of the year, many of the kids will keep their artwork and school reports to share with us when we come. These kids do not have a mother nor father that they can give their artwork for display on the family refrigerator door. I often have a hard time holding back the tears as I see drawings featuring the orphan in the middle, holding hands with my husband and me, and with our two kids holding our hands on the outside. There is always a big house in background, usually a sun shining on us, and all of us are smiling. Pictures really are worth a thousand words: these children just want a home and loving parents.

Does working in the arts interest you? Learning to paint or play the piano, starring in a play (or working behind the scenes), or serving as a docent at a favorite museum might give you pleasure. Former

President George W. Bush learned to paint in retirement. Painting portraits honoring servicemen and women has become his passion.

Is getting into shape a goal, now that you have time to take that daily walk or prepare healthy meals? I see in my own life that either I fit in going to the gym no later than seven in the morning or it just does not happen. *Healthy meal-making?* Hah! Only on weekends. Thank God there is a great juice bar next to my office with healthy salads and a Whole Foods on my way home offering healthy prepared food. It's my current reality, but one I'll turn it on its head in retirement.

Can you set aside an afternoon a week to teach a child or even an adult to read?

Can you use your business talents to advise young entrepreneurs? The Senior Corps of Retired Executives (SCORE) pairs retired business owners and execs with those at the other end of that continuum, creating amazing mentoring relationships. I suggested them to my hairdresser before he set up a new salon and they put him on the right path. SCORE is a terrific outlet for retirees and resource for the people it serves.

In a similar vein:

Can you serve on a trustee board, applying the talents, training, and experience you gained in the business world? I'm on the board of trustees and also serve on the finance committee at my local hospital, Newton-Wellesley Hospital, which is a member of Partners HealthCare, founded by Massachusetts General Hospital and Brigham and Women's Hospital. Even though I have a demanding full-time job, I believe it is important for me to make the time to give back to my local hospital.

I also serve as a member of the Partners HealthCare Institutional Review Board/Human Research Committee. Even though reviewing the protocols for proposed research takes up an entire weekend of my time each month, I feel good about giving back. Plus, the subject matter is engrossing for me, since I nearly went to med school.

What do you want to leave as your legacy? Is it physical and public, such as funding the revitalization of an inner-city park, building a new wing for a hospital, or funding a nonprofit to help children with cancer? Or will your legacy be focused more on family, such as helping pay for your grandkids' college education or teaching them about the world by taking them on trips?

If you could attend your own funeral, what would you hope to hear in the eulogy? If I died and the orphans I've helped could pay their respects, I'd hope at least a few would say, "Because of her, I went to college," or "She helped our village get fresh water."

* * *

One advantage of wealth is its ability, with wise investment management, to produce growth and income in retirement and provide both peace of mind and the wherewithal to pursue whatever purpose-driven retirement means to you.

It might be giving money, time, or resources—or a combination of these. The first step is figuring out what matters most to you. If you give some serious thought to the questions posed in this chapter, you'll be well on your way to doing so and to incorporating those things into your postwork life.

For me, purpose means paying forward my own success. In chapter 10, I'll share the reasons why in hopes that doing so might further inform your thoughts on your own purpose in retirement.

CHAPTER 10

Paying It Forward

Never doubt that a small group of thoughtful, committed citizens
can change the world; indeed, it's the only thing that ever has.

—Margaret Mead

EARLIER I SHARED the story of a pivotal moment in my life: a disastrous morning early in my first pregnancy when I was certain I'd blown my chances with a prospective client, discovered my brand-new car was damaged by a hit-and-run driver, and lost the stone in my engagement ring. Any one of these would be bad enough in one week, let alone in one day—before lunch!

Then came the kicker: a prolonged game of phone tag with my OB/GYN. It *had* to be bad news, since he'd promised to call within a few days after my amniocentesis if the preliminary test results indicated a problem.

"God, if you really exist," I prayed then, "I ask you to give me a healthy son, and I promise to teach him about you."

Months later, on the day my son was born, I gazed at my healthy child and remembered my promise—then realized I first had to learn about God *myself!* I started attending church. It reminded me why I was not—and never would be—religious. The things the supposedly pious do and justify in the name of faith upset me. I decided to learn about God on my own from his scriptures, and started at the beginning: the Old Testament.

I love reading about successful people, learning what makes them tick. Of the dozens of biographies I've read, from Andrew Carnegie to the Vanderbilts, the Rockefellers to Warren Buffett, none speaks to me quite like the story of King Solomon.

By current standards, his wealth was $2.1 trillion, much of it in gold—twenty-five tons of which, the Bible says, he received *each year* from his famous mine in Ophir and as tribute from Arab kings, who regularly sought his counsel. As King of Israel, Solomon controlled trade routes to and from Europe, Africa, and Asia. The taxes assessed and paid by the traders and merchants bolstered his wealth, which remains unsurpassed by anyone to this day. (Compare Solomon's two-plus trillion to the fortune of the wealthiest man in America today, Jeff Bezos, founder of Amazon, with a net worth of $160 billion.)

Solomon inherited the throne from his father, King David. In the Bible, in 1 Kings, chapters 2–4 you will find this account of Solomon's life:

"I am about to go the way of all the earth," King David told his son. "So be strong, act like a man, and observe what the Lord your God requires: Walk in obedience to him, and keep his decrees and commands, his laws and regulations, as written in the Law of Moses. Do this so that you may prosper in all you do and wherever you go."

The young king obeyed his father so completely that the Lord Himself was impressed. He appeared to Solomon during the night in a dream, saying, "Ask for whatever you want me to give you."

Solomon said he wanted a discerning heart, to govern his people and to distinguish between right and wrong. In short, he asked God for wisdom.

God said to him, "Since you have asked for this and not for long life or wealth for yourself, nor have asked for the death of your enemies but for discernment in administering justice, I will do what you have asked. I will give you a wise and discerning heart, so that there will never have been anyone like you, nor will there ever be. Moreover, I will give you what you have not asked for—both wealth and honor—so that in your lifetime you will have no equal among kings. And if you walk in obedience to me and keep my decrees and commands as David your father did, I will give you a long life."

God gave Solomon wisdom and very great insight, and a breadth of understanding as measureless as the sand on the seashore.

Since studying this scripture, I make it a point every morning when I pray to ask God for wisdom and discernment, as this is essential in my work of advising my clients on how to grow and keep their wealth.

The fact that the richest man to ever walk the earth asked God for wisdom and discernment clued me in to something few people seem to understand: if you possess those two things, the rest takes care of itself. Solomon realized this and lived it; his three thousand proverbs, many of which are found in the book of Proverbs, speak for themselves of his wisdom, as does the book of Ecclesiastes, written during the last years of his life.

As I mentioned in chapter 4, what I find fascinating are the spiritual laws God reveals in scripture. Not unlike the laws of physics,

I have found that if you obey or disobey these laws, there are consequences. As I found with the spiritual law of tithing in Malachi 3:10—give the first tenth of your income—the consequence is that God blesses your finances.

In the story of King Solomon, the spiritual law revealed is that if you are obedient to God's commands, laws, and regulations as written in the Law of Moses, the consequences are that you will prosper in all you do.

God outlines his spiritual laws in the Ten Commandments. If only Bernie Madoff had followed the commandment that says, "Thou shalt not steal," his clients would have been a lot better off! Plus he would not be spending the remainder of his life in prison and his grandchildren may not have lost their father to suicide.

The physical laws that govern our universe are constant and unchanging. I believe the same is true of spiritual laws. God's physical laws can be found in a physics book; His spiritual laws can be found in the Bible. Just as God established physical laws, such as the law of gravity, so there are spiritual laws that have been set in motion by God. And they are just as sure as physical laws.

Whether I believe that gravity exists or not, if I step off the roof of a building I will fall to the ground. I cannot see gravity and I cannot see God, but I believe in my heart that God is as real as gravity. Because of this, I take his spiritual laws and the consequences of obeying or disobeying those laws seriously. I have applied God's spiritual laws consistently to my life for many years now, and they never fail to produce the promised results.

I believe that scripture is the inspired word of God as spoken through Moses, Solomon, David, Isaiah, Jeremiah, and many chosen others. I believe the scripture is given as a book to instruct and teach powerful life principles. So if my goal is to give wise counsel to my clients, how do I get this knowledge, wisdom, and understanding? Chapter 2 of Proverbs tells me how.

I will share with you a few of these spiritual laws about what God says about giving to the poor and the consequences of doing so:

In Deuteronomy 15:10, it says to give generously to the poor "and do so without a grudging heart; then because of this the LORD your God will bless you in all your work and in everything you put your hand to."

In Psalm 41:1–3, seven promises accrue to those who give to the poor:

> Blessed are those who have regard for the weak;
>
> the LORD delivers them in times of trouble.
>
> The LORD protects and preserves them—
>
> they are counted among the blessed in the land—
>
> he does not give them over to the desire of their foes.
>
> The LORD sustains them on their sickbed
>
> and restores them from their bed of illness.

The Bible also gives us spiritual laws regarding prosperity.

Joshua 1:8: "Keep this Book of the Law always on your lips; meditate on it day and night, so that you may be careful to do everything written in it. Then you will be prosperous and successful."

Psalm 128:1–2:

> Blessed are all who fear the LORD,
>
> who walk in obedience to him.
>
> You will eat the fruit of your labor;
>
> blessings and prosperity will be yours.

When I got to the book of Malachi, the last in the Old Testament, I already believed in the importance of seeking wisdom. But I wanted firsthand proof of the power of God's laws, and accepted His challenge (Malachi 3:10), to test Him in tithing. A year later, (as detailed in chapter 4) we were out of debt and I'd found my purpose: giving back.

I've tithed ever since, and (perhaps unsurprisingly, bottom-line person that I am) I see it as an investment, just like any I'd make in the market: I choose carefully where to give time and money and expect good things to happen.

The many forms of good

Just as pursuing a purpose means different things to different people, doing good takes many forms.

It might mean helping someone in your family who is struggling with chronic illness, mentoring a child to learn right from wrong, or donating needed funds to researchers working on a cure for cancer.

I favor charitable organizations where the majority of my donation goes to the cause. For instance, my cancer research donations go to Hope Funds for Cancer Research, whose primary activity is to award fellowships to young researchers who have the highest probability of making an impact in the hardest-to-treat cancers and with the goal of turning death sentence cancers into chronic disease. More than ninety-three cents of every dollar donated to Hope Funds for Cancer Research in 2018 went to funding grants and grantee programs. More information can be found on their website, www.hope-funds.org.

The following examples don't even scratch the surface of the tremendous need that people who are inclined to help can play a role in filling—whether right under our noses or on the other side of the world.

My purpose in retirement will be to continue supporting causes I care about. The three whose stories I'm about to share are included here not as a pitch for your support, but to *support you* in answering an age-old question: *Why are we here?*

My hope is that the work these organizations do inspire you to see and find purpose in what I think is that question's only logical answer: *we are here to do good.*

Boston Rescue Mission

Every city has soup kitchens and shelters that serve the homeless, and Boston Rescue Mission (BRM) also provides these services (find out more on www.brm.org). But as one of the oldest rescue missions in the country (founded in 1899), it seeks to *end* and *prevent* homelessness by attacking the problem at its roots.

BRM provides job training. They have veterans' programs, a residential recovery program, and a sober living program, to name just a few. They serve nutritious meals, but the crux of the mission's work is delivering individualized help to get the homeless off the streets permanently.

I serve on BRM's board of trustees, and the president and person running the mission—John Samaan—is unbelievable. He's Egyptian by birth and started working with the poor in his early teens in the slums of Alexandria. He's also worked in Los Angeles on Skid Row. John has been with BRM for over twenty-five years. Talk about purpose. Talk about a man who has made it his life's work to help change people's lives.

All donations go right to the poor. John keeps the administration tight, and he's always out there looking for volunteers to come in and give their time—whether to serve a meal or help clean up after it. He's just amazing at getting the most out of volunteers to really keep things going.

Better than a Mercedes

After he'd graduated from dental school, which he attended full time thanks largely to my work as an operations manager, my husband, Ken, made a promise: one day, he said, he would buy me a new Mercedes-Benz. And when I turned fifty, he tried to make good on that promise.

As we walked around the dealership looking at the ridiculously priced cars, I said to my husband: "Instead of buying one of these expensive new cars, let's celebrate my fiftieth birthday by taking the family somewhere—like Africa. We'll celebrate my birthday there, go on a safari for a couple of days, but more importantly, we can do something to help out the poor and do something that makes a difference with this money."

You see, I was noticing that our children, who were close to ages twelve and fourteen, were asking for more and more things. Because Ken and I worked very hard at our professions, we were fortunate enough to live in a nice suburb of Boston where many of the high school students drove nicer cars than their teachers. The privilege of living near the top of the food chain in America can spoil a child but quick.

My thoughts were that this trip to Africa would not only benefit some people living in poverty but would also show my kids firsthand that other kids around the world have it tough—often going to bed hungry and wearing rags for clothing.

My husband ended up setting up a temporary dental clinic while I coordinated—from scratch—the construction of a new orphanage on the outskirts of Nairobi to replace a decrepit one. The children there were on the opposite end of the food chain from our own, quite literally: they urinated in bed at night because some who had walked outside the building after dark had been preyed on by wild animals.

I hired local workers from the slum behind the existing orphanage and paid them a premium, provided they worked from sunup to dusk. We all worked in the one-hundred-plus degree heat to get the building finished as soon as possible.

The lifelong connections we made and the serendipity that manifested again and again at just the right times to allow the project to be completed was, for me, further testament of the power of giving back. When you do good, I believe God clears the way and helps it happen.

It was a trip none of us will ever forget. I saw my Josh and Ashley change into more compassionate and caring children with new hearts for those less fortunate.

After that visit to Africa, when I saw how having access to fresh water could be life changing for the health of a village, I made it a point to research and find an organization with a mission to dig wells to provide fresh, clean water to African villages. I have since donated to a charitable organization called Wells for Kenya. Over the years, I have gotten to know and respect the founder of this nonprofit organization, Michael Martino, a well-regarded stained-glass window artist known for refurbishing church windows, including those of Trinity Church in Boston. Through Mike's connections and resourcefulness, we have been able to buy and ship a good number of water pump motors to villages in Africa. (Learn more about Wells for Kenya at www.wellsforkenya.org.)

Agape International

Agape (pronounced uh-GAH-pay) means unconditional love that is giving, caring, and sacrificial—a fitting name for an orphanage dedicated to feeding, clothing, sheltering, and educating children in India who have been affected by HIV/AIDS.

This organization was founded in the early 2000s by an amazing woman—and former employee of mine—Lynne Voggu. In all my life, I have never found a more compassionate and caring person. (You can learn more about Agape at www.agapeintl.org.)

While working at my company, Lynne lost her best friend to cancer. She decided she wanted to get away—not on vacation but instead to help a poor village in India. During Lynne's trip, she saw orphaned children begging on the streets; they were homeless after losing their parents to AIDS. She returned with a new purpose and the drive to do something about it.

Now, let me make sure you understand the sacrifice Lynne made to rescue these orphans from the streets. Lynne was a young, single, beautiful woman with a full career ahead of her in the financial services industry. She lived in a nice condo in an affluent Boston suburb. She was always perfectly dressed, with her heels matching her outfits, and never a chip in her manicure. She was living the dream of many young professional women.

Lynne gave it all up to make a difference in the lives of orphans. She no longer has those perfectly manicured nails, and I have never seen her wearing high heels with a matching outfit on my annual trips to India. Instead, I have witnessed and even helped her find a cemetery plot to bury a child who just died. This is not easy to do in a place with the population of India—and remember, the compromised immune system that is part and parcel of HIV means the childhood diseases we seldom think twice about in this country are often a death sentence.

I have been with Lynne as she took in a new orphan with full-blown AIDS, malnourished, with a head full of lice—and watched as she made sure this child was given everything they needed to survive and thrive. Lynne, in my mind, is a Mother Teresa.

One very difficult story sums up Agape International's importance in the lives of those it serves and in my own life. It also conveys the importance of being present for children without families.

It's a sixteen-hour flight to Hyderabad, India, and I go once each year. A couple of years ago, within hours of arriving at the orphanage, I learned that Swami, a sweet little guy I'd known since he was five, was having emergency brain surgery.

Swami had full-blown AIDS when he arrived at Agape and had now been diagnosed with tuberculosis of the brain. The surgery was to alleviate pressure on the brain caused by infection-induced swelling. It's difficult enough to fight off TB when one is healthy. For a child with HIV, it is simply impossible.

Lynne and I went directly to Gandhi Hospital in Hyderabad, a government-owned teaching hospital that employs some of the India's most-respected doctors. It is equivalent in reputation to some of the best hospitals in the US, yet it is one of the dirtiest places I've ever seen. Lights were out in the halls. People who brought in sick relatives would sleep in the filthy hallways because their villages were so far away.

Our first job was to clean the plastic mattress with alcohol and change the filthy sheets that Lynne knew, from past experience with other sick orphans, would be Swami's bedding. There was black mold on the walls of this neurosurgery recovery unit. It was filled with a dozen people recovering from surgery and crowded with visiting families. The visitors were coughing. It was hard to believe that this was where newly postoperative patients were put for recovery from major surgery.

I spent the last three days of Swami's life beside him. I will never forget praying for him and seeing tears flow down his face as I prayed. Though he could not speak and was in a coma, he clearly knew Lynne and I were there.

I still cry when I think that Swami died without his own mother or father there to comfort him. Both had died of AIDS. Yet I believe that God had planned for me to meet Swami, to show him love over the prior seven years, and to be in India to fill in the gap for his mother as he died.

If this seems a bitter memory, it is. But in its way it is also sweet. I was able to comfort a young man whose short life made my trying childhood seem like a walk in the park. A sixteen-hour flight was a small price indeed to pay for that privilege.

I believe that everyone comes into my life for a reason. I believe that God will sometimes put us in a specific place, at a specific time, for a specific person God has destined for us to help. We may not perceive the impact we have on that person, but his or her life will be better because of our touch. The words we speak and the actions we take will bring hope into painful situations.

You are important. It is possible the kind, caring words you speak may help someone who is unable to see the bright promise in his or her future. Your help may be what changes someone's life.

I am so thankful for all the clients whose lives have intersected mine. I cherish and am blessed by all of these relationships. I am hopeful that I have made a positive difference in their lives and their beneficiaries' lives.

Live Your Dream!

THROUGHOUT THIS BOOK, I have shared experiences I draw on in helping my clients protect and expand their wealth.

As we have seen, I tailor a strategy for each client based on their circumstances: what they require for peace of mind and what, beyond that basic sense of security, they hope to accomplish in their Act Two.

I hope these experiences have helped you better understand both the positives and the pitfalls you'll want to consider in choosing and working with a wealth management professional. Whatever form your Act Two takes, strategic wealth management can help assure that you have the wherewithal to pursue it.

When retirement comes, enjoy every moment. And remember: nothing feels better than doing good.

I truly believe that's why we're here.

To do good.

About the Author

DEBRA K. BREDE is the founder and president of D.K. Brede Investment Management Company, Inc.

A Barron's Hall of Fame advisor, Debra has been helping high-net-worth individuals, business owners, and retirees pursue their financial goals for more than thirty years. She began her career working within the traditional Wall Street business model but soon realized that investors weren't being treated fairly by firms that too often put sales goals ahead of clients' needs. So, in 1990, she founded her own independent practice, D.K. Brede Investment Management Company, where her clients have always been her number-one priority.

Starting from humble beginnings and holding firm to her beliefs, Debra has become nationally recognized as a top financial advisor by numerous publications, including *Financial Times*, *Forbes*, and *Barron's*, which has named her among the Top 100 Women Financial Advisors nationwide for fourteen consecutive years. She is also a frequent media commentator on investment-related topics and has been featured in *Barron's*, the *Wall Street Journal*, the *New York Times*, *Businessweek*, *Bloomberg*, and *Kiplinger's Personal Finance*, *and has made appearances on* CNBC, Fox Business, and NBC Nightly News.

Debra is involved with local and global charitable organizations. She was one of three finalists for the 2015 Invest in Others Global Community Impact Award in honor of her work with Agape AIDS Orphan Care in India. In addition to serving on Agape's board of directors, she and her husband, a dentist, travel to India each year caring and providing for the orphaned children with HIV.

Debra is a graduate of the prestigious Harvard Business School Owner/President Management Program.[9]

---

9   Barron's Top 100 Women Financial Advisors bases its ratings on a pro-prietary analysis of the following qualitative and quantitative criteria: a minimum of 7 years of financial services experience, acceptable compli-ance record, client retention, assets under management (AUM), revenues generated, and the quality of the advisor's practice. A portion of the ranking considers a sampling of a financial advisor's clients. Please note that this is not representative of any one client's experience. Barron's does not provide a count of eligible nominees for the award, citing its data as proprietary. Investment performance is not a criterion. The listed awards and recognitions are not indicative of the wealth manager's future per-formance. Barron's 2019 Hall of Fame Advisors recognizes advisors who have ranked for ten or more years on any one of the following Barron's Top Advisor lists: Top 100 Financial Advisors, Barron's Top Women Financial Advisors, or Top 100 Independent Advisors. Please visit www.bredeinvest-ment.com for more information and disclosures concerning this and other awards referenced.

Services

DEBRA BREDE OF D.K. BREDE INVESTMENT MANAGEMENT COMPANY is affiliated with Commonwealth Financial Network® member FINRA/SIPC, a Registered Investment Adviser–broker/dealer. Through Commonwealth, she offers securities and advisory services, including investment advising, financial planning, estate planning, tax planning, risk management, and investment services for high-net-worth individuals.

Founder and president Debra K. Brede, along with her team, builds custom investment portfolios for the firm's clients, selecting holdings that target specific financial goals and emphasize each client's long-term objectives. Assets are managed with a consistent focus and discipline, which are key to pursuing successful investment results over time. As with the construction of a fine suit, the care and attention to detail with which Debra crafts each client's investment strategy are reflected in how well it fits the client, whether he or she is accumulating assets before retirement, spending assets in a tax-advantaged and strategic manner during retirement, or planning for the efficient transfer of assets to the next generation.